# And The Money Will Follow

## 29 Ways in 29 Days to Change Your Finances Forever

Tama Borriello, CFP®
Financial Advisor

And The Money Will Follow
29 Ways in 29 Days to Change Your Finances Forever

Copyright © 2009 by Tama Borriello
Published by Leading on the Edge™ International
704 228th Avenue NE #703
Sammamish WA 98074
leadingonedge.com

ISBN-10: 1-933750-21-9
ISBN-13: 978-1-933750-21-7

# And The Money Will Follow

# And The Money Will Follow

*"We must be willing to get rid of the life we've planned,
so as to have the life that is waiting for us."
~ Joseph Campbell*

In the early 1990's a young woman was on the precipice of graduating from the University of Washington. She was focused on one goal; to launch and build a new business and had a small fortune of $25,000 to do so! Surprising everyone in her life, it was one of the one percent of start-up businesses that survived.

Fast-forward to a decade later and successful business co-ownership with her then husband, marriage and mothering. In her focus on the big picture of management and success, she never expected all that had been built to not be there forever. As many of us have experienced, or *will* experience, life can hand us the unexpected sometimes. That woman was me, and when my life took a detour, I found myself as a single mother who was exceptional at building and running her own business as well as exceptionally remiss at balancing the long-term financial and social realities that women face.

I have written this book, and work as a Certified Financial Planner and Financial Advisor, because I am committed to helping women and men find the tools they need to make wise and balanced personal and financial decisions, whether, in the words of Joseph Campbell, we have the life that we planned, or the life that is waiting for us.

Over the past few years I have often revisited the success and balance that characterized what I did before I knew what I was doing. I was singular in my desire to launch my own business and have the ability to call the shots in my future career. I kept decisions simple. If something didn't work, I found the fix, did it and moved on. Once an interviewer asked me what my biggest mistake had been. I was stymied for an answer because I couldn't think of a "mistake," instead I honestly answered, "Well, lots of things don't work out, so you just try something else." I had a zest for life and people who made me look forward to each day.

Over the past few years, I've also revisited some of the catalysts that encouraged me to start wondering why smart, hard-working, educated people like me, as well as my friends, employees and colleagues, were so unaware of the details of living balanced lives. I had weathered divorce, forensic audits, and single parenthood, even buying a failing business and turning it around. At the time of my life detour, I felt that although I had experienced some years of imbalance I was now back on track. I had no concept of how off track I had veered.

Have you ever found yourself off track, or feeling out of kilter? It can either promote change or disaster! The final year of owning my last business included memories of my disappointed daughter at a school tea party I missed because I couldn't tear myself away from my business, frustration at not being able to do a good job in managing the details of my personal investments and a general feeling of drudgery. As my kids (and Austin Powers) would say - I had lost my "mojo," my zest for life.

After all my hard work, I felt like I had merely bought myself a job and had no quality of life to show for it. I was exhausted, stressed, and unpleasant. In focusing on the grand goal of building my own business, I had neglected everything that was truly important to me. The irony of simultaneous financial success and a complete inability to enjoy it was not lost on me! To this day, I still encounter financially successful women who are utterly unable to enjoy their lives. I noticed that several of the women I respected and cared about also juggled family, social and business obligations haphazardly.

At that serendipitous time, a business broker in a three-piece suit walked into my company carrying a cash offer from an executive who wanted to buy my small business concept. It was the kick in the seat of the pants that I needed to understand my mission in the life. I sold the company and took a year off. I began to research all the issues that had coalesced into such a personal interest.

During that period of my life, I found that when you spend a major portion of your time reading about and talking to women from all walks of life about how to live a balanced life, you start hearing the similar themes. What I heard made me realize that I was not the only one who had experienced difficulty. Many women are trying to figure out how in the world they achieve their best destinies, and live satisfying, balanced lives when they are faced with the primary responsibilities of care giving to children and extended families, coupled with the desire to create successful careers and legacies and manage their financial lives.

I discovered that some of what I had already experienced and more of what awaited me down the road - the pull between work and life- inevitably leads to shortchanging one or the other. The reality check for women is that they often have some unique variables that directly impact their ability to save enough for retirement. In fact, now more than ever, it is essential for women to take charge of their financial lives.

Would you like to venture a guess on what percentage of women experience conflict among the major roles they fill of caregiver, mother, wife, and employee? According to the 2003 Caregiver Resource survey, it was 96 percent. Aside from the 11.5 years they statistically take off to raise children, women also represent 75 percent of the caregivers to elderly family members. The average age of widowhood is 56. Nearly 50 percent of women will go through a divorce. On average, women earn about 81 percent of what men earn, and they work at jobs for shorter periods of time (which affects pension and retirement savings eligibility). If women divorce, nearly half of them experience significant reductions in their standards of living. Women not only need to save up for an extra 10 to 15 years of outliving their spouses, but many are passionately committed to social goals, education and financial stability for children, families and parents.    All of these statistics add up not only to a woman whose financial life changes far more than a man's, but if she lets it, fear-based decision making and ultimately, a life out of balance.

I assert that the time is now for women, at any stage of their lives, to get their financial houses in order.  Let's contemplate turning the tides to balance.  We can only fulfill our personal, social and financial goals if we come from a position of confidence and strength.  I have found, from countless women, a lack of confidence in making the decisions necessary to manage the many-faceted areas of their lives.  This lack of confidence can lead to short-term and fear-based choices, or living a life that is merely a facade.

In a joint study in 2005, Heinz Family Philanthropies and WISER Women (Women's Institute for a Secure Retirement) found that women in the U.S. between the ages of 30 and 55 were not adequately prepared for retirement.  This lack of preparation stems from pay inequities, occupational segregation, care giving responsibilities, longer life expectancies and women's work patterns.  These issues result in reduced pension earnings, public benefits and personal savings.

Did anyone ever give you the book, "Do What You Love and the Money Will Follow"?  That's a great book, but guess what:  doing what you love does not give peace and balance to a mom trying to pay her household bills, save for college, and pile money into a 401k plan!

When you are under the gun, you make survival-based decisions for the here and now.  The psychologist Maslow wrote in his hierarchy of behavior, that unless you have satisfied survival and safety issues of yourselves and the ones you love, you can never go on to the higher levels of self esteem, self knowledge and self actualization.  There are ladies we each know and care about, and— surprise!  --  some of the most successful "on paper" businesswomen, who need to figure out how to balance the competing objectives in their lives before they can start to deal with the details.

I would like to share some daily concepts I've applied to my life which have resonated with many of my clients, friends and colleagues. I have perceived that the reason many women have not embraced fulfilling their personal, social and financial goals is **not** because of lack of passion or ability, but because of a combination of societal, cultural and educational issues.  Training your mind to begin making millionaire-planning decisions will be a process that takes place over time.  The secret is that changing small decisions made each and every day will eventually add up to massive changes in your personal financial life.  If you want to have a lifetime of sound financial planning, setting aside a few minutes each day to check in on your spending and investing habits or to enhance your understanding of the financial world will become one of your trusted routines for making excellent decisions. As you embark on this journey, remember that small differences at the start can result in dramatic differences later on.  29 Ways in 29 Days will get you started on the path to change your finances forever.

And The Money Will Follow

# Getting Started

# Day 1

## What's Your Legacy?

*"There are certain things that are fundamental to human fulfillment. The essence of these needs is captured in the phrase 'to live, to love, to learn, to leave a **legacy**. The need to live is our physical need for such things as food, clothing, shelter, economical well-being, health. The need to love is our social need to relate to other people, to belong, to love and to be loved. The need to learn is our mental need to develop and to grow. And the need to leave a **legacy** is our spiritual need to have a sense of meaning, purpose, personal congruence, and contribution."*
*~ Stephen R. Covey*

Although it may seem counterintuitive, the first step to creating balance in your current life is clarity as to what you want at the end of, figuratively speaking, the "day." Do you remember a time in your life when you were "in the zone"? Stop for a moment and envision it--maybe a sport, a work project or a string of successes in your area of expertise. It can best be described as a rare calm in which you operate at your highest levels of consistency and productivity.

Olympic gold medalist, Wendy Boglioli, once shared with me the story of the day she won her gold medal at the Montreal Olympics. She described in detail waking up, the beautiful weather and flowers, her father's meaningful presence, the food she ate and the overall sense of clarity she felt on the day that she and her team staged what is still known as one of the greatest upsets in Olympic swimming history. She had spent years preparing for that moment and had focused all her energy on one purpose. While the great athletes and achievers of our generation may define their "end of the day" goals as gold medals, fame and glory; we will each have our own definitions of what we value. That is what today's small change in perception is about. Focusing on two or three goals of what you want your life to look like will allow you to single-mindedly make decisions and operate in the zone now and in the future.

What is vital right now is to quickly and without thought record the answer to the following questions. What is most important to you in your life? What three or four items spring to mind? What do you want said or remembered about you at your personal end of the day--even your funeral?

Perhaps you would like to be remembered by your community as a member who cared deeply about the quality of the town and its children. Perhaps your legacy includes what your own family remembers about you. As you go through this thought process, write it all down--stream of conscious-ness. Don't worry about too many entries or thinking fantastically.

What is most important to me in my life?

_____

_____

_____

What do I want said or remembered about me?

_____

_____

_____

From this exercise you will want to discern the two or three most important areas of your life goals and legacy. You will each have your own individual approach to leaving your imprint on the world, but at the end of this creative exercise, you will find that you have simply created the guidelines to your life map. Refer back to this "map" to help you make critical decisions when going through the rest of the 29 day guidebook and beyond when planning your time, your days and your life.

As we all know, making changes from habitual behavior can seem impossible or incredibly challenging. That is why I've asked you to create an actual written list. Copy it down and carry it with you, hang it on your computer, your refrigerator or wherever you spend a lot of time. For a while, I found several creative ways to remind myself to stay on track. I fashioned computer passwords to remind myself of my goals. I wore an unattractive rubber band around my wrist (then quickly upgraded to a snappy bracelet!) so I could snap myself whenever I forgot to consider the most important thing--my legacy. I encourage you to take whatever creative steps you can to help you remember what you want to change.

Corporate poet, David Whyte, wrote about the importance of relishing work in our short lives. After devoting half of a lifetime to science and ecology, he began to realize he was not fulfilling his true desire--his life legacy. He wrote that the hardest part of his life change was explaining to his father-in-law that he was quitting his well-paid job as a scientist to become a poet!

The list you have created will be a lifeline when planning for all elements of your life that need to be balanced--even your career. Whyte wrote a lovely book about seeking fulfillment in your occupation entitled, "Crossing the Unknown Sea--Work as a Pilgrimage to Identity." In it he stated, "Our bodies can be present in our work, but our hearts, mind and imaginations can be placed firmly in neutral or engage elsewhere. Being engaged elsewhere can be damaging to our souls."

How liberating to see work not only as a means of support, but also as a means for fulfilling one's legacy. At one point in the book a monk makes the simple observation that the antidote to exhaustion is not rest but "wholeheartedness." Ideally, we want to be wholehearted in every area of our life. Let this legacy list be a helper to you as you embark on finding and creating work that is, to paraphrase William Blake, both right for you and good for your world.

As you are looking back over your legacy list that you wrote with no judgment, you may feel as if some of your goals are insurmountable or difficult. Do not let that dissuade you from your list. Instead look to the next day's way regarding miracles.

Three common themes I see reflected above in my legacy list:

1. _____

2. _____

3. _____

# Day 2

# Physical Health + Mental Health = Financial Health

*"Life is no brief candle to me. It is a sort of splendid torch which I have got a hold of for the moment, and I want to make it burn as brightly as possible before handing it onto future generations."*
*~ George Bernard Shaw*

Before we go any further, I want to ask you a question: For your three or four legacy items, did you enter something along the lines of "physical and/or mental health"? The first few years I kept this list, I'm embarrassed to say I never thought to put physical or mental health on my list! It did not seem like a priority when I was devoting myself to raising two children, building a vibrant business and just surviving.

Sanjay Gupta, the CNN Senior Medical Correspondent, wrote a book entitled, "Chasing Life." In an interview Mr. Gupta talked about the origins of the book. Originally he wanted to write a book about immortality and the new upcoming age when technology will outwit death. He was planning on exploring the implications of the "fountain of youth". Something funny happened on the way to his potential bestseller. He found himself repeatedly drawn to the fact that our world right now knows a great deal about living life to the fullest and ultimately living longer and healthier lives. He found that in repeated interviews, there was not much interest in living forever, or thereabouts, with any type of compromised lifestyle. Rather, most people were very interested in living their lives, in his words, "like an incandescent light bulb, burning brightly, until they suddenly go out--no flickering at the end." What he discovered changed his entire impetus for writing his book and living his life. He changed his research to the concept of "health span" or the number of healthy years we live.

Can you guess how much of our life span comes from genetics? According to overlapping scientific, health and philosophical studies, the way we live our lives and the daily health choices we make account for 70 percent of our life span. Genetics accounts for only 30 percent. So we can blame grandpa and grandma for a small percentage of our current health situation, while knowing that our outcomes emanate from our many daily choices, both small and large.

This realization inspired Sanjay to start living well with the goal of being there for all of the important events in his family's future, spanning the generations. He stated that, "Living well now is like putting money in a savings account. The dividends will come later, as you age. The better you are at saving, the richer you will be when it comes time to reap the rewards."

So before we go any further, let's do a quick evaluation of where we all are on life span! Answer the following 10 questions with true or false:

1. I get more than 30 minutes of exercise a day.
2. I can always find time to work out.
3. I usually prepare healthful meals.
4. I eat sweets and junk food in moderation.
5. I generally get enough sleep, even if I'm busy and trying to save time.

6.   When I'm stressed I take time off.
7.   I am currently pursuing a passion of mine.
8.   I regularly connect on a daily basis with something bigger than my day-to-day concerns, like nature, meditating or service to others.
9.   I have and keep an annual appointment with my doctor and dentist.
10.  I tell my doctor everything about my health habits and family history.

If you have ten "true" answers, congratulations on living a healthy life. If you have even only a few "false" answers, add as your number one legacy goal "physical and mental health." Without that, you won't be able to, or be around to, fulfill your deepest legacies, goals and dreams.

The ultimate fuel, as you strive to live a balanced life and fulfill your legacy is to give the importance due to your health. Knowing that to fulfill your legacy you need a nutritious diet, daily aerobic and weight bearing exercise and lowered stress will help you prioritize this vital goal--personal health and well-being.

The knowledge that a positive outlook on life and sense of value to your family and community contribute to a healthy body can be a powerful influence in helping you make the hundreds of daily decisions regarding what you put into your body and how you take care of yourselves and your psyche. This profound sense of purpose may create far more change in your diet, exercise and self care choices than any diet fad that promotes external appearance, rather than your overall health.

I read that the average American has to make over 200 food-related choices a day! Add that to all of the other decisions women must make, and having a legacy life list to refer back to will cut out a lot of the confusion. For example, if I lose a big account today, will a stop at the donut shop help me in my big picture goals? Or if I consistently have to deal with a client who pays me well but makes me feel terrible about myself, should I fire the client and improve my mental health or let them continue to tear away at me and the goal of fulfilling my legacy?

**The daily choices to treat yourself badly either through food, exercise or emotionally beating up on yourself are infinite. Just think if every time a negative situation or a difficult choice presented itself, you trained yourself to reflect back to your LEGACY, your very reason for living, and ask the question, "What best fulfills my legacy here?" It is a massive change in our response and ultimately, your decision making process.**

Today I will revisit my "Legacy List" realizing that in order to achieve my goals I must honor my own well being first:

Three ways I will honor my own well being in order to fulfill my legacy list:

1. _____

2. _____

3. _____

# Day 3

## Make Things Happen

Have you ever read a great self-help book, or heard an inspiring speaker who made you feel like you were on the road to achieving your goals? The ideas and concepts offered were guaranteed to help you get the results you wanted in your life. Then, a few weeks later you realized that nothing much had changed for you? It is so hard to make wholesale changes in one's personal habits that entire books and studies are devoted to understanding why it is so challenging for humans to break bad habits, or implement new ones.

In an "O: The Oprah Magazine" article written by Martha Beck, she told the following story. "Recently, while paging through an old journal, I rediscovered a daydream I'd written down years ago. It described my fantasy backyard, a desert oasis with natural plants, a rock garden, areas paved with natural stone. A surge of amazement and gratitude overwhelmed me. The description matched the backyard I actually have right now. I'd connected with my heart's desire, and the desire was fulfilled. Miraculous!" In the article, Martha then recalls some other important facts surrounding this story. For starters, the 38,000 pounds of rocks and gravel she had delivered to her once barren backyard. Then she noted the months it took for her to personally shovel, trundle, rake and arrange all of it.

What Martha Beck discovered is the less advertised side of miracle/changes. It is having the impetus to make the changes we desire in our lives and the will power to carry them out. In my time as a financial advisor, I have heard statistics and stories about the fact that more than fifty percent of inherited funds that may have been accumulated over decades are spent within three years of transfer to heirs.   It is the core reason New Year's resolutions are usually a bust.   It's why we can listen to a life-changing speaker and feel a profound change in our heart then walk right back into our normal routine an hour later.  I already know as I'm writing this guidebook that relying on one's personal determination and tenacity may not be enough of a catalyst for change.  The reason why is that we humans have evolved to seek safety.  If we are alive and well, although we may not like where we are, we'll choose time after time the comfort of the habitual and the known.  In order to break free from mediocrity and live the life one dreams of, it is imperative to change the everyday "habits" surrounding the areas that one seeks to transform.

Let's talk about how to change your habitual behavior.  If you are committed to putting your life on track for powerful financial changes you must begin to rewire your brain on a daily basis.  That is why we started this guidebook by listing the three most important guiding principals of what you want to accomplish in your life.  As noted in the physical and mental health section--seemingly inconsequential, yet negative habits can be changed when we put them within the context of whether they support our legacy.

To change your basic patterns of living, set aside a few minutes every day to visualize reaching your legacy goals.  Also, begin to create opportunities to stick to your changes: (1) Give yourself a small task each day, (2) schedule it into your routine and (3) make it too convenient to pass up.  For example, if you are trying to keep track of your spending, have a basket or file where you walk in the door and put down your bags.  Immediately throw your paperwork in the file. The first step to the process is done and was quick and painless.

Implementing these changes may take time, but don't despair as studies have shown that it can take a number of weeks to mentally change ones engrained routines.

Here are some suggestions to implement on a daily basis:

- Organize your financial files (taxes/years/important documents/financial statements/etc.) in a convenient locale near where you pay your bills making it easy to quickly put your important papers away.

- Set up your financial information so it can be easily viewed in a five minute check-in each day. That way when you log onto your computer in the morning it's an easy choice to get in the habit of checking in on your on line finances. Use one of the many free and secure "my accounts" functions that banks and brokerage institutions now offer to their clients. This will allow you to efficiently and quickly monitor and reinforce your commitment to understanding and monitoring how your money is working for you.

- Leave a file folder right where you walk into your home and file receipts, old statements, etc.

- Create a file for all of your daily cash receipts so you can track and understand where your money is going.

- Use a convenient monthly budget that tracks all bills, as well as your monthly cash expenditures by setting it up in a place you use every day, like a computer or a pad of paper near your daily organizer.

- Set up an area that is only for working on your finances. Have an inbox for statements, bills and a filing system within hands reach.

As you begin to create the foundation for your financial miracle, begin to make those changes little by little. Use failures as an opportunity to think of what does work for you, as opposed to focusing on the lack of initial success. The most sophisticated financial planning and self help books in the world will not help you until you can train your brain to follow the path you desire. If you are committed to millionaire planning, rather than merely interested in winning the million dollar lotto, then you will find yourself incrementally doing what must be done to reach your legacy.

Here are three things that I can do immediately that will make my millionaire planning part of my daily routine:

1. _____

2. _____

3. _____

# Day 4

## Know Where You Stand Today

*"We all know how the size of sums of money appears to vary in a remarkable way according as they are being paid in or paid out."*
*~Julian Huxley, Essays of a Biologist, 1923*

In order to get your financial life ready for future success you **must** know where your money is going now. The prospect of gathering and tending to the many details that make up your financial life may seem overwhelming, or not that big of a deal. You are changing your finances forever after all! The only way to take control of your legacy and propel yourself to financial security is to understand the impact of the small daily decisions you make in your life. Once you have a handle on those, you will be able to make concrete plans and goals that you can stick to.

To fulfill your personal legacy be sure to perceive daily, monthly, and yearly budgeting as a way of life, not a one-time project. It is one part of the vital foundation upon which your legacy will be built. While you may start with making incremental daily changes, be aware that to succeed you must address budget and financial organization as an ongoing lifetime project. Visualize it as an exciting project to get where you want to be financially, not as drudgery even though you may have your own misconceptions about keeping a budget and acknowledging where your dollars go.

The reality is that many of us were never given the foundation for sound budget planning. While we may have committed the diverse elements of managing and paying for our busy lives (schedules, kids, meals, extra activities) to memory, our time strapped culture does not encourage us to take the time to record this information, or keep it in a place of importance where we can refer to it (other than affixed to the refrigerator!). Have you ever been involved in building your own home, or responsible for a big work or charity project? As you may recall, none of these projects starts without a blueprint or a plan that outlines how it will be built, or the preliminary planning necessary for the project to be completed. We spend years in the quest to become educated, become specialists in our careers and live successful lives without any detailed emphasis on the spending side of the equation. Just as you built a foundation educationally and occupationally to get to where you are today, you need to ensure that you have a basic plan as to where all of the benefits of that work, portrayed in dollars, is and will be going. Investing the time to create and understand that plan will establish the bedrock upon which the rest of your decisions will be based.

Assembling your balance sheet is the next crucial step to financial change. Not only will it help you organize and direct your resources but will then lead you on the path to realizing your Legacy Goals that you listed on day one. One important note: the following spreadsheet is intended to guide you in recording simply and quickly what you know about your personal finances. It is meant to help you get started on the path to financial fitness. When you turn the page, don't get bogged down in details. As you go through the planning day by day, you can always return to revise this portion.

Today I will record:
1. What do I own?
2. What do I owe?
3. How much do I make?

# Personal Balance Sheet

| Assets (What I Own) | Total |
|---|---|
| Banks, Credit Unions, Cash | |
| Investments (taxable) | |
| Investments (taxable) | |
| Retirement Plans | |
| Retirement Plans | |
| Benefit Plans (pensions) | |
| Benefit Plans (taxable) | |
| Real Estate | |
| Personal Assets | |
| Other | |
| **Total Assets:** | |
| | |
| Liabilities (What I Owe) | Total |
| Credit Card Debt | |
| Consumer Debt (auto) | |
| Home Mortgage | |
| Other Mortgage | |
| Home Equity Loans, HELOCS | |
| Student Loans | |
| Loans against life insurance or 401K | |
| Other | |
| **Total Liabilities:** | |
| | |
| **Net Worth** **(Total Assets minus Total Liabilities):** | |
| | |
| Other Assets | Total |
| College Savings Plans | |
| Trust Accounts | |
| Cash Value of Life Insurance | |
| Other | |
| **Total Other Assets:** | |

| Cash Inflows (How Much I Make) | Total |
|---|---|
| Partner "A" | |
| Partner "B" | |
| Interest Income from CD's, money markets | |
| Dividend Income from taxable accounts | |
| Rental Income | |
| Annuity Payments | |
| Trust Income | |
| Social Security Income | |
| Pension Payments | |
| IRA Income (required over age 70) | |
| Other | |
| *Total Cash Inflows:* | |

# Day 5

## You Feel Like You Need a Miracle

Never forget, miracles don't just happen, each one of us can "work" our own miracles. The operative word here being "work"! I've kept many of my journals from the time period of my life when I was changing my career focus to something that held true meaning for me. Journals are an amazing way to witness momentous changes over time that we may not realize ever occurred. If many of us look back on our goals and dreams from 10 or 20 years ago, we can see the results now.

You may have heard the story of the founder of the nonprofit organization, Washington Women in Need, Julia Pritt. I have had the pleasure of hearing her story several times. Fifteen years ago she had just gone through the end of a long-time marriage, breast cancer and the death of her mother. **Instead of focusing inward, she focused on her legacy.** Her own experiences made her realize how difficult it would have been to go through difficult times without the resources she had. She started WWIN to benefit low-income women who needed a helping hand in getting back on their feet. It took over a decade, but miraculously she created an organization from scratch that went from helping a few women a year to over 3,400 in 2007.

Or, maybe some of you remember the headlines in the late 1980s and early 1990s when AIDS became a prominent theme, which the media, for a time, associated with certain social and ethnic groups. Mary Fisher, a prominent and politically active conservative, made a speech at the 1992 Republican convention in which she shockingly not only announced that she was HIV positive, but began to lay out her legacy for helping those afflicted with the disease. What was she doing in 2007? She's still running her nonprofit organization that helps AIDS victims from all over the world. What a miracle! Who could have imagined a mom from American suburbia visualizing and creating a major, international nonprofit company?

Einstein said, "There are only two ways to live your life. One is as though nothing is a miracle. The other is as though everything is a miracle." I believe we do not have to worry about whether miracles exist or not, we can be confident in knowing that we can create miracles through our own commitment and single-minded focus. Today is the day to contemplate your legacy list and believe that each item is and will be attainable through your focus and hard work.

Today I will remember three amazing miracle-type occurrences I have already experienced or want to experience:

1. _____

2. _____

3. _____

# Day 6

## Keep it Simple

*"Besides the noble art of getting things done, there is the noble art of leaving things undone.  The wisdom of life consists in the elimination of non-essentials."*
*~Lin Yutang*

Why do I add such a seemingly inane principle to financial success? Two words:  experience and observation.  I look back on my own experience as a young businesswoman and remember my intuitive approach to keeping it simple.  As the years pass, our perception of simple and perfection may go awry.  As a savvy woman professional, I was an expert at running my own specialized businesses.  I knew I had the ability to understand and do many things, as well as a bit of skepticism regarding others' advice being better than my own, so my perfectionism kicked in and I attempted to micromanage many areas of my life.  For years, I thought it was just me, but the more conversations I've had with other professionals, the more I realize perfectionism is a weakness that many succumb to which only takes them away from their core competencies, and in a worst case scenario is used as a type of psychological avoidance to truly realizing their full potential.

The reason it's included in this portion of the guidebook is as a simple hint to not let this work towards getting your financial life on track get waylaid by perceptions of trying to do everything perfectly, or being overwhelmed by the task at hand. If you find yourself at a roadblock as you seek to fulfill your goals, make sure you are "keeping it simple" in your quest.

Without going into the underlying issues as to why some of us fall prey to micromanagement, I propose a simple approach. I once read a magazine article on micromanagement (so I could deal with it from others--ha!). The slow chill I felt was my simplicity-oriented Irish grandmother's voice yelling down from heaven, "Tama, keep it simple, sweetie." I was pretty sure that article was written about me - I was guilty. I was not keeping anything simple in my false efforts to insure success in my business and family. Not only was I letting my fear of failure or making a mistake force me to do all sorts of things that were not my expertise, or even my responsibility, but also it was affecting my business success and relationships with my employees and loved ones.

In an article on this subject by human resources expert, Estienee De Beer, she wrote, "Just like Clark Kent goes through a telephone booth to become Superman, micromanagers need to learn how to transform themselves into leaders of people. They need to learn not to over-intellectualize tactical issues and avoid getting into a stupor over statistics. Leaders focus relentlessly on simplicity and empowerment."

How do you want to be remembered? If you want to achieve balance and success in realizing your life legacy, then the concept of focusing on simplicity needs to be applied to every arena of your professional and personal life. If you have challenges implementing this concept, it may require some mental work to set up the foundation of delegating.

As a business owner, I sometimes received terrible advice from various professionals. When I was given excellent financial or professional advice, I often did not recognize it. I hired people to do things in a hurry, since I myself was out of balance. I vacillated in decision-making, tried unsuccessfully to do many things myself and neglected my core area of expertise. Frankly, it was my inability to manage all of the facets of my life and keep it simple that drove me to get out of my last business. It was only when I was on my self imposed sabbatical that I understood what was holding me back, along with many other women, from success.

A few years ago, I read a Business Women's Network article called "WOW Facts" that stated that women spend 40 percent more time than men researching a fund before they invest. Wow. That sounds astute. As a financial advisor, it means that my women clients may be more thoughtful and more risk-averse than men when it comes to investing. From your viewpoint as women professionals, mothers, wives and community volunteers, can any of you imagine what else those women could be doing with that time? While I am a tremendous advocate of financial literacy for women, the reality is that if you want to achieve success you must focus on your core competencies and goals. Women cannot spend their lives researching and finding the best statistical answer to every area of their lives. They must use that 40 percent more time cited in the study to research the very best financial, professional and personal partners to support them in their quest for balance.

We're all good at the process of research and analysis. Let's apply that on a grand scale to keep our lives simple:

Find partners--financial partners, childcare partners, anything-that's-not-your-area-of-expertise partners. Once you've laid the foundation of research and analysis, trust them, oversee them and focus on your goals. Is it a perfect solution? No, you may not always choose the right person or solution. However, that is part of being human--you learn from your mistakes and move on. Your ultimate goal is to surround yourself with partners who are just as vested in your success as you are. For example, I consider myself a CFO to each of my clients. I advise them on comprehensive wealth management strategies, business liquidity sources, their credit and lending needs and sift through many investment ideas and present the best to them. I'm paid a flat fee to do so. That's my core expertise and I do it well. All of my clients know that I am 100 percent committed to their success, since my referrals and future growth of my business is linked to them. Something I know how to do, but don't have the time for, is insurance needs. I work with an insurance agent who is well versed on every product out there, analyzes the best company, uncovers needs I may not have thought of and is 100 percent committed to my success since she values my personal business. Could I do it myself? Yes. Is it my core expertise? No. Consequently, I choose to invest my time, my life energy, in the area that is my core competency and trust other carefully chosen partners to help me manage other areas of my life.

Focus on your core expertise and farm out the rest. Maximize your current income to create opportunity to balance your life. Consider that you may be purchasing family time, or quality time. By approaching the management of your life with the concept of simplicity, you can maintain balance and provide the best professionally to your colleagues and clients and the best personally to your family and loved ones. Keep it simple!

Three ways I will simplify my life so I can concentrate on what I do best:

1. _____

2. _____

3. _____

# Day 7

## Enjoy the Present

*"You could wake up dead tomorrow."*
*~Homer Simpson*

As you are going through this daily process of getting your financial house in order, remember the most profound concept to apply to each area of your life, financial and beyond. Today is the only guarantee you ever get in life. Ever. Anna Quindlen, in her book, "A Short Guide to a Happy Life," wrote, "Knowledge of our own mortality is the greatest gift God ever gives us, because unless you know the clock is ticking, it is so easy to waste our days, our lives."

After the period of my life I call the "divorce and life detour," I bought a failing retail and wholesale food service enterprise. I knew I had the capability to turn the business around and make it profitable. I threw myself headfirst into exactly the type of behavior that had created the imbalance in my life in the first place. I also moved within a few miles of my opinionated Welsh grandmother whom I loved dearly, but I still didn't see her any more often. In the midst of a successful, busy holiday season, I didn't have much time to really enjoy more than a few hours with my family. My Christmas gift from her was a slender book about enjoying the gift of the present. I thought it was sweet and didn't look at until after her quick passing away a few months later. It was the same eerie chill I felt when I read the magazine article about micromanagers. I could suddenly picture that little Welsh lady up above, shaking her finger at me and saying, "Wake up Sweetie, the clock is ticking, and you have no time to waste."

In Quindlen's book she notes that we should each think of our life as a "terminal illness." A friend of mine thought that seemed extreme. She asked, "Should we go around all depressed since we're about to die?" Anyone who has read Paulo Coehlo's book, "Veronika Decides to Die" will chuckle at that notion. Once the suicidal Veronika found out she was going to die, she suddenly wanted to live more than anything in the world! No, in answer to my friend, we should live our life each day focused on what's truly important; fulfillment, passion and unconditional love. My grandmother's subtle message has nurtured an increasing understanding of the fulfillment and happiness that can come from purposefully living the lives we dream of.

The self-imposed time-wasters of doing things because we "should" that do not fulfill our legacies, micromanaging areas of our life in order to maintain an illusion of control, energy wasted on regrets over mistakes made, feeling sorry for ourselves and not being willing to make a miracle work, suddenly become obvious wasters of time. Why should we invest our precious time and energy in debilitating thoughts and beliefs when our time here is limited?

The gift of understanding that our short lives have an investment perspective as well, and that it is represented by our time, spirit and love, helps us single-mindedly begin to select how we will spend those items to manage the balance of the days we have left and carry on our legacies.

Remember the theory about making miracles happen, but we may have to work for them. Recently one of my first and favorite clients commented on the circle my life has come to. I've met and married an amazing man, am sharing a vibrant and full life with all of our children and manage a business as a financial advisor to clients I care deeply about. She said, "What a miracle for you." I'll tell you the real miracle in my life--the ability to live each day as a terminal illness, to make decisions based on a few simple facts, to keep it simple, to realize my legacy because this is not practice, but real life, and to realize that I will still make mistakes and to cut my losses and move on, and in fact, embrace mistakes. The quicker I learn a lesson the quicker I can get back to effectively attaining my goals. After all, life is terminal.

The most satisfying part of living a life focused intensely on making the most of your short time here and honoring your closest values and wishes is that you begin to invest your precious time in things that add more balance and fulfillment in your life because you are choosing what fulfills you and satisfies your very legacy of living.

As we define our legacy, with the concept of a limited time on earth in mind, we will lose interest in comparing possessions, money and accolades with other people's lives. When we're faced with the myriad of daily decisions necessary to run our lives, but that also need to honor the balance between our personal, social and financial goals, this concept will support us in removing habits, relationships and jobs that deplete the resources we want to devote to attaining balance. In the words of Anna Quindlen, "Live deeply every day and from your own unique self, rather than merely to exist through your days."

## What am I investing my time, spirit and love in right now?

1. _____

2. _____

3. _____

## Are these areas consistent with my legacy list?

# Day 8

## Planning for Couples and Partners

*"Treasure the love you receive above all. It will survive long after your gold and good health have vanished."*
~ *Og Mandingo*

Married, partnered or not, this guidebook is designed to help apply simple repetitive concepts and habits to help achieve your own vision of financial success. It can be applied to an individual, a couple or even a family. Applying these principles to a lifetime partnership can reap more than just monetary rewards. Operating with full financial disclosure and cooperation leads to clarity and true intimacy in a relationship.

We go through many phases in our lives. Something a couple agreed on at one time that became a pattern of financial behavior may now lead to a dead end road in reaching their changed goals. However, finding the impetus to make changes to a plan that has already been followed without major disaster (or sometimes even with disaster!) can be downright impossible. Recently, in an effort to preserve the location of a TV in our bedroom, my husband offered to change who sleeps on which side of the bed. It seemed like such a little thing (especially in light of the fact I was angling for the departure of the TV) that I agreed to the switch without thought. During our month of the "switch" as we now refer to it, neither of us could sleep and tossed and turned trying to get comfortable. We were both thrilled to return to our traditional side of the bed. I realized that if we couldn't even change sides of the bed, how could we or any other couple broach changing the spoken and unspoken financial roadmaps that had been decades in the making. A major financial change may go beyond an obvious goal such as saving more money, to the loaded questions of what gets cut in order to save more money. Just like growing a miracle garden, it requires loads of work, water and fertilizer!

The Work Part - It is vital to communicate with honesty and affirm your past cooperative successes while exploring future possibilities. This is a challenging foreign land to navigate, evidenced by many studies that place money as the biggest culprit for marital arguments and even divorce. While there are a myriad of cultural and emotional beliefs we each cart into a partnership from our own parents and upbringing, I have found that the same steps that can get an individual on track through first defining legacy goals, then creating a road map for how to get there, can help partners begin to chart their course as well. As you go through the work, address your goals, current target spending allocations and changes without emotional judgment. If you find yourselves road blocked, use it as an opportunity to re-visit your legacy goals and your common interest in getting there.

The Water Part – Get out of your normal environment. Take a weekend trip to someplace you love; meet with your advisor and pair it with a fun lunch date. Find ways to tell each other exactly how you feel in a judgment free environment and be sure to show appreciation for your partner's honesty to you as well. Remember, there are always win-win solutions. There never has to be a win-lose. Be willing to brainstorm ways to find compromises between differing goals or viewpoints.

The Fertilizer Part – Do not discount the value of a good bottle of wine or favorite celebratory food or drink to commemorate successful compromises and even attempts at making changes.

Although you may want to avoid it, keep sharp by agreeing to sit down monthly and quarterly; check in to see if you are following your plan.

Goals & Ideas for:

1.  The work part:

_____

_____

_____

2.  The water part:

_____

_____

_____

3.  The fertilizer part:

_____

_____

_____

# Financial Planning 101

# And The Money Will Follow

# Day 9

## Find an Advisor

*"Investors have very short memories."*
*~Roman Abramovich*

*"Fools think their own way is right, but the wise listen to advice."*
*~Proverbs 12:15*

As I look back on my life, I can think of several expert advisors who have guided me along the way. Just as the value of a mentor in our day-to-day lives cannot be understated, neither can the value of having a professional and objective financial advisor to help build and implement an investment plan. While you may encounter hundreds of different sources of expert advice, there is no substitute for the advice of an individual who has taken your legacy goals, the facts about your family and your inner fears and hopes and reframed those within the context of recommendations intimate to your life. Beyond having a knowledgeable professional who is alert to market trends, changes in tax and retirement laws and keeping watch over your portfolio details, a financial advisor can serve as a trusted and dispassionate source of advice--both what one wants to hear and what one does not want to hear.

Your top three considerations in finding an advisor are credentials, ethics and business philosophy. As for credentials, the gold standards are the CFP® designation (which stands for Certified

Financial Planner™) or a CPA with a Personal Financial Planning Specialty. Financial Advisors who hold the CFP title have taken a two-year course of additional study, have at least three years of industry experience and have to pass a challenging, two-day, board certified exam, testing their expertise in a wide range of financial planning and investing topics. (CLU; ChFU)

To learn more about an advisor's integrity and ethics, research his or her background on the Financial Industry Regulatory Authority website (www.finra.org). Pay particular attention to the personal referrals that people you trust (as well as your accountant or attorney's referrals) may make to an advisor with whom they have worked. Do not hesitate to ask questions and be wary of a potential relationship with someone who uses terms that are difficult to understand or that you do not feel comfortable communicating with. Even if you find the most lauded financial advisor in the nation, it is equally important to be able to communicate and have clarity about each recommendation made.

To discover more about an advisor's business philosophy, discuss his or her planning process and viewpoint about investing and managing your financial life. There is value in choosing a financial advisory team with different areas of expertise and credentials in accounting, investment planning and portfolio management. After doing your research, meet with potential advisors in person. Look for an advisor who is compensated in only one way--through fee based planning. That way a negotiated fee keeps you and your advisor on the same side of the table. There are no commissions or other factors that might cloud the perceptions of the objectivity of the advice given. Take the time to search for an advisor who creates a written plan outlining how he or she will help you reach your goals, how objectives will be implemented and how your investments and investment plan will be monitored. Make sure the advisor is comfortable consulting with the other professional advisors in your life such as your tax or legal consultants. You are building an A team to insure that the best interests of you and your family are being met. Remember, a goal without a plan is just a wish, so you want an advisor with a process that helps you create a strategy to reach your goals.

Taking the above steps will give you the ability to manage the rest of your life with your full attention on your areas of expertise and interest, knowing that you have hired and advisor with the know-how to oversee and competently advise you on your entire financial life.

If you don't have a financial advisor or financial mentor now, start asking people you trust and respect who they would recommend. If you already have one, check in and see if they are on track to provide you the guidance and planning you are seeking to undertake.

Name three people or professionals that I trust to ask for their referral advice:

1. _____

2. _____

3. _____

# Day 10

## Create Your Financial Plan

*"Good plans shape good decisions. That's why good planning helps to make elusive dreams come true."*
*~ Lester R. Bittel, The Nine Master Keys of Management*

Welcome to the core of this guidebook. Here's where you will take all the work you've done so far in recording your personal legacy goals, organizing your paperwork, and recording your assets, liabilities and budget and create a preliminary plan that guides you along the path to having an effective investment plan.

Why do this part, if you have already organized your goals and financial life? Isn't it the key to financial success to be on top of things and know what you ultimately desire? Nope, that is not enough. In my own life, and in my practice, I have found that people don't fail to meet their financial goals due to one poor choice. Rather, it is often a combination of emotionally based decisions and/or complacency that prevent them from meeting their expectations, or as Lester Bittle notes, "to make elusive dreams come true." In fact, I'm still amazed by the number of people who are entirely surprised and disappointed regarding where they ended up in both their financial and personal lives, even though they never made a plan to arrive anywhere in particular.

46

I remember a time in my former life when I was at the top of the world in running my own business, master of my financial information and was sitting at home one night, literally surrounded by piles of cash. It was utterly heady and my then husband and I had a list of items we wanted to buy and things we wanted to do with all of our material success. I proceeded to bungle along for a few years feeling "rich" and living a corresponding lifestyle. If I wanted a new car, I bought one. If I read an article about bag ladies I would fearfully not spend money on much of anything for a few weeks. I would try out an investment idea that felt good, without understanding anything more than how high of a return it might have. Some ideas worked out, some didn't! After a decade or so of that behavior, I had to ask myself why I hadn't arrived at the pinnacle of financial security that I had assumed would be my ultimate destination.

The hard truth is that if we don't plan on where we will arrive, we will never get there. We'll arrive somewhere; although there is no guarantee it will be by choice. Having a legacy based financial plan takes emotionalism and short-term fear-based thinking out of the decision making process. This plan will give you a road map to guiding the small and the big decisions for the rest of your life.

Today is the beginning of building out your plan. Each day we'll focus on a different aspect of your personal finance planning. For starters, think back on your legacy goals. In order to reach them, what needs to take place with your finances? Do you want enough of a nest egg to take time off from work and volunteer for something you care passionately about? Do you want to be financially "free" at an earlier age than regular retirement age? Do you want your children and/or grandchildren to never have to worry about paying for education? In order to fulfill your legacy life dreams and goals do you need to build up your savings, understand where your money is going, earn more on your investments, spend less money or even be more accountable to yourself?

Look back on page one at your legacy goals. What step(s) do you need to take financially in order to meet each goal?

Legacy goal #1:

_____

_____

_____

Steps to meet the goal:

1. _____ by: _____

2. _____ by: _____

3. _____ by: _____

Legacy goal #2:

_____

_____

_____

Steps to meet the goal:

1. _____ by: _____

2. _____ by: _____

3. _____ by: _____

Legacy goal #3:

_____

_____

_____

Steps to meet the goal:

1. _____ by: _____

2. _____ by: _____

3. _____ by: _____

# Day 11

# Forget About Your Budget!

*"Give me a stock clerk with a goal and I'll give you a man who will make history. Give me a man with no goals and I'll give you a stock clerk."*
~ J.C. Penney, Founder and CEO of JC Penney

Financial Planning analyzes your income, expenses, assets and liabilities today, and then analyzes the income, expenses, assets and liabilities of your future. It then meshes all of these numbers with your hopes, dreams and goals and helps you to create a road map to get from point A of today to point B of where you want to arrive. It will guide you if you become confused, tired, lazy or fearful, as well as enable you to confidently open the door to opportunities that may come your way.

You've already been paying attention to your budget and assessed where you stand financially on your personal balance sheet. You have a clear idea of what you own, what you owe and what your income is. Today is the day to completely dismantle any past perceptions of budgets that are either automatic approaches to paying your bills, or that sound like they require you to deny yourself and live a sparse existence. Brace yourself; you've just been appointed Chief Financial Officer of Your Life, Inc. Just like any successful corporation that allocates money to different areas to grow their revenue, you will create a spending plan goal that invests in items that are consistent with you fulfilling your legacy goals and living a healthy, well thought out life. If you feel like your monthly income is so high that you do not need to spend time exploring your monthly cash flow, I would advise you to reconsider. Understanding where you allocate your resources is a valuable foundation to translating the rest of your financial life and meeting your goals down the road.

In my past life as a business owner, I would create unique "guerilla marketing techniques" (that is, advertising with not a lot of money relative to the corporate business giants of the world!) I would garner visibility and good vibes for my companies in order to generate more income. It might include sending samples of our products to the decision makers who might hire us as a supplier or mailing out postcards with memorable pictures about our family business to the local neighborhoods. Although low rent ideas, they still cost money and had to be carved out of our business-spending plan. I also had to allocate rent payments, salaries and the myriad of daily expenses to keep our business thriving. Without fail, when we invested in each area of our spending plan, we benefited. Our landlord made sure our space was well taken care of, our employees came to work knowing they would be paid, utilities, water and heat came on to light and heat our world and our business grew as people heard about us or tried our products and wanted more.

That is how you will look at your monthly spending plan (forget that old fashioned budget), you are now building a successful enterprise, "Your Life, Inc." and need a great spending plan to get there! First you need to account for the basics of living and necessities, then account for expenses to protect yourself in case of the unexpected (emergency fund) and catastrophes (insurance) by allocating funds towards those items whether they occur in a given time period or not.

Then there is your CEO pay. "Who?" you might ask! Well, in addition to being the CFO, you're also the Chief Executive Office of Your Life, Inc. (congratulations!) You are the person who needs to be paid first in order to fuel your enterprise. You may have heard the adage, "pay yourself first" in various financial self help books. What I never understood is how I could pay myself "first" when I had a mortgage, dependents and legal liabilities to pay. Here's the rub: the concept is right on. If we don't intentionally carve out a way to pay ourselves, we'll never achieve the level of savings and personal investment that will help us arrive at our desires. How do we surmount this obstacle? By devising a spending plan based on your goal of investing in your future.

Today you will take your old budget and turn it into a spending plan. You will list what you intend to invest in lighting, heating and nourishing your corner of the world and then list what you intend to invest in your future life. This spending plan will target only where you must invest your resources, or desire to invest your resources. If you are passionate about your daily latte and want to invest three dollars a day for it, that is your choice. If you find you are not so passionate about it, it won't make the cut and those dollars will be invested elsewhere. Make this list without judgment or concern for amounts that seem too large or small. This is designed to be a starting point as you examine whether and how you are spending your capital consistently with your goals.

# My Spending Plan

| Spending for your Corner of the World | Total |
|---|---|
| Housing | |
| Utilities | |
| Food | |
| Transportation | |
| Emergency Fund | |
| Insurance: | |
| - Healthcare | |
| - Auto | |
| - Life | |
| - Personal & liability | |
| Debt | |
| Education | |
| Taxes | |
| Health | |
| *Total:* | |

| Spending for the Future | Total |
|---|---|
| CEO Pay | |
| Retirement Investment | |
| Entertainment | |
| Social Activities | |
| Eating Out | |
| Developing talents | |
| Investing in Others (Charity) | |
| *Total:* | |

Today, after recording where I will invest my resources, I will commit to investing the following amounts, no matter how small, to my "Spending for the Future" plan:

1. CEO Pay _____ $ _____

2. Retirement Investment _____ $ _____

3. Excess Debt Payments _____ $ _____

# Day 12

# The Spending Plan and Debt

*"If you think nobody cares if you're alive,*
*try missing a couple of car payments."*
*~ Earl Wilson*

While there are more seemingly logical areas of your spending plan to address first, often debt can be the 500-pound elephant in the room, so let's just tackle it first. There is good debt and bad debt, and if you have a lot of the former, you can instantly identify with the idea of a 500-pound elephant in your living room. No matter where you are on the debt spectrum it is vital that you understand how to use "good" debt to your advantage and how to stay out or get out of "bad" debt."

If you want to grow "Your Life, Inc." into the vibrant goals of your future and feel great about your current allocations into maintaining your corner of the universe you must approach debt with all the discipline and single-minded concentration of a Navy SEAL. I do not use this comparison lightly. Being unable to control one's spending habits, or getting in over your head with debt can undo your chance of ever fulfilling your legacy goals. Think back on the spending plan you just created--the plan where you chose to invest your resources. How did you feel when you saw the end result? If the sight of the dollars that must be allocated to credit card or consumer debts was frustrating in that it wasn't going over to the "Spending for the Future" column, or just plain overwhelming, then the only way to get over this obstacle is to approach it as a tactical military undertaking. Understand the enemy, plan out your method of defeating it and undertake it without hesitation.

Our country and consumer-oriented culture are no help when it comes to making good debt decisions. We are a nation of debtors, who recently encountered even more trouble with the ability to take out gobs of debt based on, at best, our home equity, and at worst merely a signature. If you don't have the money to pay for items in the here and now, why finance something that you will end up paying far more than its material value, and infinitely more than the value those dollars could hold invested in your future.

Bad debt is paying interest that has no tax advantages and/or is a higher rate than you could earn by investing the dollars in order to purchase goods that depreciate in value. Good credit comes through purchasing a home (and sometimes other real estate investments) that appreciate in value over the long run and offer tax advantages and financial leverage.

While dealing with credit and debt problems is beyond the scope of this guidebook, if you need to take a detour and research debt consolidation, zero percentage credit cards and cleaning up your credit, do it first and foremost or you will never be able to completely fulfill your life legacy goals. If you have a manageable, but unappealing pile of debt to deal with, create a hierarchy of what gets paid off first and a plan to do so. Higher interest rate debt gets paid off first (while maintaining minimum payments on any other loans and credit). Remember, while chipping away at this goal, it is still imperative that you pay your CEO too! Even if it's a nominal amount, you are incrementally changing the way you manage your life on a daily basis, so the very act of allocating even only a few dollars to "paying yourself first" is a solid first step to the vast sums you will be paying yourself in the future.

If you are faced with assuming college debt for your child consider the fact that while your kid has years of earning ahead of him or her, you do not and there are no "retirement loans" for us folks nearing full retirement age!

If your monthly debt (net of mortgage) divided by your net income is around 10 to 15 percent, you're O.K., but know that zero "bad" debt is what will give your spending plan the power to invest in your future appreciation, not past depreciation. If you are wondering how to craft a millionaire plan out of the simple spending plan you've just created, after making today's plan regarding debt, read on!

Today I will make the following plans to understand my debt choices, systematically get rid of bad debt and follow a disciplined plan going forward regarding my spending choices. I choose to invest in my future.

## Debt Deliverance Plan:

1.  List of bad debt:

   _____

   _____

   _____

2. Go back to previous budget page – how much will I allocate to paying off bad debt each month?

_____

_____

_____

3. When considering incurring additional debt, look at your legacy list...does that debt fulfill any of your legacies?  Look at day seven – are you investing in what is most important to you?

_____

_____

_____

4. Keep repeating until debt goes away – re-visit often if this is an issue in your household.

_____

_____

# Day 13

# The Spending Plan of Life

*"Have nothing in your houses that you do not know to
be useful or believe to be beautiful."*
*~William Morris*

If your spending plan seems difficult to follow, or if you feel that
you cannot allocate as much as you desire into investing in your
future, you have just been handed a glorious opportunity:   the
chance to sit back and consider how you are investing your life
energy (money from your work) into the daily schedule of your life.
On an even more profound level, this is an occasion to consider
what gives you long lasting internal pleasure, as opposed to
immediate gratification.

Implementing your spending plan will allow you to consider how to
balance your present enjoyment with your future pleasures.   This
plan will actually give you the ultimate control and ability to
consciously choose what and how you live. Now that you have a
better idea of how much income is coming in and how much of your
energy, oops, I mean cash, is going out, you can take a clear look
at whether your spending behavior is supporting your legacy goals.
Look back on those legacy goals you listed on day one, and as you
implement your spending plan and observe your in-the-moment

decisions regarding cash flow, begin to ask yourself whether an upcoming purchase or activity enhances and expands your legacy. Turning the prosaic daily choices we make at every juncture into life-changing decisions regarding our future personal fulfillment can be an illuminating, and perhaps profitable, way to guide your life.

You may find that you are investing more than you ever realized on small items that add up quickly and that you really don't need. The "latte factor" taught in a popular financial advisory series has become common lore, as many of us have taken time to add up our little habits and calculate how much of a yearly investment we are making in seemingly innocuous purchases.

When I first began to build my financial planning practice, I would reward my long hours with a daily afternoon trip to the coffee shop for my favorite fancy drink and the pastry du jour. During one low cash flow month I happened to use my visa for nearly all of my incentive trips. The following month, sitting uncomfortably in pants that were becoming too snug, I took a look at my Visa bill and thought there was some sort of mistake. I eventually added up nearly $300 in small charges from the lovely baristas downstairs. Could it be that I was investing $3,600 a year in the afternoon equivalent of tea and crumpets? Could it be that I was gaining a few extra pounds in the process and hadn't noticed the cumulative effect on my cash flow and waistline? Yes, I was behaving like a mindless frog, wallowing in the warm water and never noticing the increasing heat. What is ironic about that time of my life is that I desperately wanted to take my daughters and myself on a vacation, but didn't have "enough" money. It was then that I started to actively try to meet my legacy goals by asking the question,"Does this invest in what I truly desire?" before expending my resources.

In this networked age, it could be anything from seemingly inexpensive downloads, music, snacks or other mindless things we consume or collect. The spending plan won't dictate what you can invest in, but it will guide you to invest in items that are truly dear to you or that greatly enhance your lifestyle. It will be your choice to decide if you would like to reallocate from one momentary pleasurable sensation, to knowing that you are funneling those funds instead to paying off bad debt, or investing in your future. Eating out, entertainment, buying things and clothes you love are fine, but just be aware of your choices.  As you rethink your perspective, you may find yourself feeling just as fulfilled to invest a $100 in the "Your Life, Inc." account, as investing it in a new pair of jeans.

In the effort to get one's spending aligned with ones legacy goals, there can be the perception that spending is a negative.  Don't fall into that trap.  From a dedicated shopper and an observer of the markets, I believe spending is a marvelous thing in our civilized world.  It is part of the cycle of life and our global economy that makes so much of our modern world possible.  The secret is to use your expenditures to support YOUR life long goals and passions, not to be mindlessly swept away in temporary, meaningless consumption.

Today I will choose three spending (investing) areas that DO support and enhance fulfillment of my future legacy goals.  I will feel 100 percent committed to spending for those items and joyous that I have the resources to commit to this area of my plan.  If faced with any other outflow decisions, I will first ask if they support my legacy.

# (Investing in others and developing talents)

Today I will choose three spending (investing) areas that DO support and enhance fulfillment of my future legacy goals. I will feel 100 percent committed to spending for those items and joyous that I have the resources to commit to this area of my plan. If faced with any other outflow decisions, I will first ask if they support my legacy.

1. _____

2. _____

3. _____

# Day 14

## The Spending Plan and Emergencies

An instructor for an elite unit of emergency responders was discussing the unplanned events that require focused intensity that he and his unit must be able to call upon in order to save lives. As he talked about the mental fortitude they are each trained to possess, he also mentioned that in an emergency situation, the typical physiological response of a human is to shut down non-essential uses. One of those actions defined as unimportant is blood flow to further off regions from our hearts, like fingers. In an emergency, our digits can turn into clumsy pieces of wood. This expert on how a body reacts under stress has had his family practice calling 911 with the phone unplugged over and over so that if they ever need to make that crucial call, how to reach out for help will be ingrained in their subconscious.

As I read that story, I marveled at the similarity to the reactive behavior I have observed in friends, clients and myself when the unexpected happens in a personal and/or financial situation. While not as immediate as a life threatening emergency, there is a similar shutdown or disconnect in doing what one should do when things go wrong versus what may feel like the right thing to do, due to fears and emotions. While it makes no sense to be standing by for a catastrophe, it is incredibly sensible and considerate to equip yourself and the ones you care about to deal with the uncertainties of life.

For the "here and now" crises, that means having important contact information, medical details, and insurance coverage available. Since you have already gathered your financial statements, located important information, key contacts (banker, financial advisor, insurance agent, attorney and accountant) and organized all of your holdings, it will be easy right now to enter that information into one contact location (document organizer follows) for a loved one, or you, to know where to go for guidance or help.

For the more long-term financial situations that can have a massive impact on your investment planning, there are some planning steps you can take that will allow you to stave off financial hiccups, or even ruin, by mitigating the impact to your long term plans and give you some breathing room during a potential financial Armageddon. Taking thirty minutes today to create a strategy to handle a job loss, a long illness, or other unwelcome event could prove to be one of the best investments you ever make, and a safe haven during the midst of an otherwise confusing time period that will buy you some time to make decisions that preserve your security for your lifetime.

The Emergency Fund was an entry you may have noticed on the spending plan on day 13, listed on the "must have" non-discretionary side of the list. While it is a no-brainer to have money set aside for emergencies, and many people are aware of it, some are reluctant to allocate a monthly amount for it. It is easy to start to consider it as a savings account to be spent in one fell swoop on a big purchase item; others use it as a monthly cushion for their cash flow. In my work, it has been asked why should one put money in a place that is not working for them, as it should be invested in a cash fund (not the stock market, that may go down right when you need the money or a bond that would tie it up, possibly when you needed it but an easily accessible, safe bank deposit). Having that money available in case the unthinkable happens, or just to even out the ebbs of flows of life can be worth a 100 percent return if it is there when you need it. Things do happen in life and if you have strategically set aside some funds to cover lost income in case you lose your job, it may allow you to look for the job you prefer instead of taking whatever you must in order to survive. It could buy you the time to spend with a loved one in illness, it could take worry off your mind if you have to pay for, and endure unexpected medical situations. Most importantly, it will give you a buffer that avoids taking funds out of a retirement account that would incur penalties, taking a loan against a retirement account, or having to take on debt at the worst possible time for you.

The emotional impact of dealing with the unforeseen changes in life, health and finances is another aspect of emergency planning that I believe is important to address before one is in the midst of loss. When one has to deal with change and their expectations have been severely altered regarding the make-up of their lives, there can be a corresponding reaction that may be soothing in the short term, but may be detrimental to their future fiscal environment. I have spoken with and worked with survivors of a death in the family who felt the dual pain of losing the center of their world, and also experienced a compelling need to fill that loss with something, they just didn't know what. For some it has led to regrettable purchase and lifestyle decisions that are difficult and expensive to undo.

If you ever find yourself going through a time of grieving, having a list of the following items may be helpful.

Let this time of planning your spending allocation to your emergency fund also be a time of planning for that fund to be your defense for a period of time that allows you contemplation and recovery with no pressure to make quick decisions.

Today, I will list the following:

1. Whom should I call for advice regarding any big money decisions or life change decisions or to help me stick to a six-month moratorium after a traumatic event on spending?

_____

_____

_____

2. What areas of my community, friends and family can I increase my investment of personal time as I recover emotionally?

_____

_____

_____

# Day 15

## Insurance Planning for Catastrophes

*"I don't want to tell you how much insurance I carry with the Prudential, but all I can say is: when I go, they go too."*
*~Jack Benny*

Still on the subject of surprising events in one's life, today we will explore how to leverage protection for you and your family by being a smart insurance user. By "leverage" I mean that if something bad happens to you or your family, you've contracted with an external group to pay most of the costs. It's no fun to pay insurance bills for your entire life, especially if you never use it, but again, if you do need to draw on insurance, even one time, it can be the best investment you have ever made.

If you are part of a partnership (marriage or business), care for children or other family members, then you need life insurance. Most likely you just need "term" insurance that expires after a certain time period. If you are worth more than estate tax limits, some would argue that "whole" life insurance has some merits. Term life insurance is less expensive and is typically suitable for most people. "Whole" life insurance builds up value over time, but is more expensive. If you are trying to decide between the two, it is worth discussions with not only a trusted insurance agent, but also your accountant and your financial advisor. Generally, the rule of thumb is that most need a policy worth five to ten times their annual income. Be sure not to overlook insuring a stay at home spouse since a nanny (and more!) would need to be hired to take their place as well.

After making sure that you have purchased enough life insurance to impart those dependent on you so they can live life without you and have their needs provided, and assuming you've already taken care of health, home and auto insurance let's talk about some often overlooked catastrophe planning, that is statistically very important to each of us.

What happens if you live, but can't earn income? Your quality of life, financial security and retirement planning just took a radical turn. The reason disability insurance is more expensive than term life insurance is that the insurance companies figured out that the odds of their customers using it were higher than their life insurance kicking in. That's right; disability is far more likely to hit you than death. While you may be thrilled to be alive instead of the alternative, plan ahead for how you will handle this sort of change in your life. From a long-term illness to an outright disability that impairs your income levels there are plenty of group plans available through many companies and disability plans for the self-employed. Warning, these may be expensive, but don't let that dissuade you from good planning. One note is that when choosing a disability insurance, be sure you've carefully reviewed and understood what the insurance company defines as "disabled" – it should be you being unable to perform your career or job specifically (you may not be able to practice as an attorney, but you can still file, obviously a step down in income, so insure for your specific line of work). Another facet to disability planning is insurance to contribute to your retirement plan (after all, if you are not earning an income, you will not be making qualified retirement contributions). If you can afford it, that is an interesting rider to add to a disability policy and again requires the input of the financial professionals in your life.

What happens if you need long-term care for the rest of your life? While it has been reported that the average long-term care user only uses the insurance for three years, what happens if you need it for much longer? The important element to long-term care insurance is to consider the financial impact on the healthy spouse. Again it is a means to care for your family if one of you should need care or treatment for an injury, illness or loss of functional capability. At this time, it is most cost efficient to buy long-term care insurance when you are in your late fifties. This is the time when, relative to your age, you can pay rates based on your health rating that may be more optimal than a few years later.

Last but not least, a very simple add-on comes along with your homeowners or auto policy. An "Umbrella Policy" protects you in addition to your basic liability coverage. We live in a fairly litigious world, so in the interest of good catastrophe planning, try to insure yourself and your family for enough to protect your assets. There are a couple of areas to keep an eye on with this type of insurance. Ask if you are getting the "full face value" of the policy, meaning that the plan doesn't just cover you for the gap between your homeowners or auto policy and the face amount of the umbrella coverage. Also ask if you have "drop-down" coverage. This type of liability will protect you in arenas that your original policies may not.

I will review my insurance and catastrophe planning with both my financial advisor and my insurance advisor:

_____ by: _____

_____ by: _____

# Day 16

## Windfalls, Good Karma

*"I find that the harder I work, the more luck I seem to have."*
*~Thomas Jefferson*

As you are looking at today's title, you may be wondering why there is a section devoted to what to do with unexpected cash windfalls that may come your way. Well, we're not only planning for the catastrophic unexpected occurrences, but also for the wonderful gifts of fortune that flit unexpectedly into our lives. If an endowment of cashola lands in a person's lap, plenty of studies have shown what happens--it doesn't sit there very long. The same sort of short-term thinking that may occur in an emergency can also rear its head in shocked excitement with positive surprises. That is why, just like we've planned for the worst, we'll plan for the best to insure that you make excellent decisions.

Sometimes "lucky" occurrences don't come in one fell swoop. We may find ourselves in an ongoing and positive change in our income or asset values and plod along, with no awareness of the fact that good fortune is visiting us and we need to either make it feel at home or take good care of it. When I was in my mid-twenties, running three small businesses, with more income than I had ever dreamed of, I had very little appreciation of, how incredibly lucky I

70

was, despite all the long hours and hard work, to experience such success. Consequently, it was difficult to plan what to do with my good fate. I look back on all of the money I frittered away, and have often marveled to others, in retrospect, that if I had just had good guidance, I would have invested more, saved more, or created a more meaningful life. Well, instead I acquired some life experience, a career I care passionately about and the impetus to write a guidebook for others on how to plan for the best.

If you have an immediate chunk of cash show up, the first rule is to take your time before doing anything with it. Second, rely on the solid investment plan you've created through this handbook.

First take a look at your assets and liabilities. If you have any "bad" debt, now is the time to pay it off or start chipping away at it. With this in mind, if you happen to receive a few hundred or thousand dollars unexpectedly you will know right where to "invest" it. If you have money left over, then take a careful look at your spending plan. What were the items listed on the "Spending for the Future" side? Now is the time to put your financial gift into things that mean the most to you. These are tied directly to fulfilling your legacy goals in life. If you are not sure how or how much to allocate to each area, assign a numerical rating to each item, with 1 being the lowest priority and 10 being the highest. For example, I personally know that having enough money to retire on and fulfill my legacy goals is my top priority. While I also want to save more money for my daughter's college costs, I know that I have an obligation to take care of myself first, so I can then take care of others. (Every parent reading this may be having a flashback to traveling with their children on a plane – same principle.) So, any windfalls that come my way are being invested directly into legacy goal number one. If you have no bad debt, have an emergency fund set aside, are on track for your retirement and/or legacy goals, then you may also want to consider allocating to a charity or cause you care about (remember that bit about taking care of good fortune when she comes to visit?).

Today we will list the three areas where any windfall money that comes our way will be invested. Later in the guidebook we'll talk about how to invest these famous funds.

I may have a windfall coming my way. Although I will be thrilled and want to buy a new (car/trip to Hawaii/pair of amazing rhinestone boots) I will patiently remember what is most important to me in life and invest in my own legacy that will be remembered far longer than the above listed thrills.

## What will I do with a windfall coming my way to fulfill my legacy goals?

1. _____

2. _____

3. _____

# Day 17

## Planning for the Unexpected

*"There is a strange charm in the hope of a good legacy that wonderfully reduces the sorrow people otherwise may feel for the death of their relatives and friends."*
*~Mighel de Cervantes*

The legacy we leave our loved ones is more than financial. It ranges from the gift of being attentive when someone is in a dire medical situation, to having the details of one's last moments and even death already provided for and on to the birthright of peaceful family relations after death. These will be the memories that surround your final days, so why not do all you can to make these positive, thoughtful times?

I once observed a meeting with adult children whose parents had recently passed away. Their frustration at their deceased parents' legal firm and financial advisors was palpable as the implications of the lack of planning their mom and dad had done in the arena of estate taxes, divvying up important family items and lack of provisions for their much loved grandchildren became apparent. It eventually became clear that their antagonism was misplaced as the truth unfolded that in actuality their parents had opted out of any planning, and choose to let "things sort themselves out." I have often reflected on the fact that that family probably had a good life, did everything they thought they were supposed to do in raising a family and maybe felt that a passive approach was fine. The true end result was that one of the final memories surrounding their passing was frustration and irritation of siblings over an extended period of time. In another meeting with a patriarch and his wife, he said, "I don't care if the government gets my money; my kids were raised to be self-reliant." I simply asked him what he wanted his children to remember about him when they were gathered around the same table we were sitting at as we sorted out his assets. He said, "I want them to remember I am 100 percent committed to each member of our family having a great education, I want them to remember the charity in our community that we've spent years building and supporting, I want them to remember how much their mother and I loved them." There was the answer, and we began to build a plan that fulfilled the legacy that he and his wife dreamed of leaving behind.

As you can see, a will is vital even if you feel like you don't have the worth level to justify one. Creating a will not only sends a message to your heirs of what is important to you, but also gives an orderly way to sort out possessions and assets. If you don't make this choice, the state will make it for you. Items that have importance can be left to whom you intended, with no difficult memories of siblings fighting over them. If you have young children, this is your chance to clarify who you want to raise them and who you trust to be the executor of your estate. Again, if you don't choose these powerful people in your children's lives, the state will, and it may not be who you intended. If you have a special needs person or parent that you care for, be sure to plan for them as well. Special needs planning has many tax and benefit implications and definitely requires the input of legal professionals who specialize in this area.

Wills are important even if you don't have children, or are not married, as you may want your assets to go to a significant other instead of your parents (which is where they would legally be directed without a will).

While estate planning is very important for tax planning reasons, it is also a fundamental foundation to protecting your assets both during and after your lifetime. While it most likely will only apply if your assets exceed a certain level, this is an area to invest the time and money for professional advice. This is your one occasion to celebrate your legacy after the fact. As the people you love are remembering you, they will also see that you have done what you could to enhance their future by your intentional planning. What a gift to leave behind.

A medical directive will ensure that your wishes are carried out in case you can't communicate. Don't overlook the importance of this easy document. None of us, at any age, are immune to the unexpected. A Medical Directive is a cross between a living will and a medical health care proxy. On one hand it communicates to medical staff what your desires are in different medical situations. For example, would you want to receive life-giving nutrition if you were brain dead? On the other hand, it clarifies who in your life has the authority to speak on your behalf. If you do not have this it can create intense dissension and guilt among those you love as they argue over what decisions are right for you. Instead, this allows the most important people in your life to understand your wishes in case you become seriously ill and cannot communicate. In many states these forms are available at hospitals, some can be found online and only need to be signed, witnessed and notarized. You can have your doctor and/or hospital keep them in your file (a bank deposit box should not be the only location, as it may not be available on a timely basis to your loved ones). Again, a powerful gift of peace and compassion to leave behind for those you love.

If you are intending to consult an attorney on a will, you can also have the medical directive and other important intentions recorded at the same time. When you are finished be sure to let key family members or friends know where those documents are located.

Today is the day to evaluate or plan for a will, medical care directive and if applicable, do your estate planning. You may need to contact legal professionals and your financial advisor for advice. Don't delay.

Write letters to those you love telling them how much they mean to you. Explain your last wishes.

To fulfill this goal I need to take each of these steps, one at a time:

1. _____ by: _____

2. _____ by: _____

3. _____ by: _____

# Day 18

## Taxes

*"A person doesn't know how much he has to be thankful for until he has to pay taxes on it."*
*~Author Unknown*

I will make this short and sweet. Taxes are needed to run this great country of ours, and you will need to pay them. How much you pay will completely depend on your strategic approach and proactive planning. If you take the time to complete your tax return and understand each line, or have a professional do it for you, it will give you some good foundational guidance for future tax planning. I am not a tax advisor. If you have questions regarding taxes, please consult a tax professional.

Have you ever finished your tax return and found out you were getting a nice big check back from Uncle Sam? Didn't that feel great? That is poor planning. You've just given an extended, interest-free loan away with YOUR money. Federal income taxes are calculated based on varying rates, depending on your salary, taxable interest, bonuses, investment income and even unemployment income. Keeping in mind that as you earn more, the increasing amounts are taxed at higher levels, you may be able to find ways to shrink the amounts that are taxed.

First, any monies you contribute to a qualified retirement plan, if you are within the income limitations, are not taxed. If you own your own business, you have some healthy options for putting a large amount towards your retirement, and shielding that income from taxes at a time when you may be at your highest tax rate.

Second, any monies you contribute to a Roth IRA are not taxed in your retirement, but give you zero tax deduction for current contributions. If you have any opportunity to contribute to a Roth IRA, or convert an IRA into a Roth IRA, double check with your tax advisor as it may be a great idea. This gives you another way to diversify your assets between types of taxation. We may not know whether taxes will be higher or lower when we retire, but having the option of withdrawing funds from your savings accounts that most benefit you at the time is part of a solid tax planning strategy.

A quick note on any tax deferred, or future tax free investments is that, unlike your taxable investment account, you will not pay tax on any capital gains or mutual fund distributions. Rather, these accounts will have the benefit of tax free, compounded growth for their life, which is quite powerful when you are considering that these accounts may be working for you for decades. You will be taxed on all of these investments, except the Roth, at your ordinary income tax when you start withdrawals.

Third, within the realm of your taxable investments you will incur capital gains taxes, or pay taxes on dividend or interest income earned. This is another occasion to lower your taxes by thinking ahead. The system is designed to reward long-term investors, meaning that if you hold your investments for at least one year, you then qualify for a lower rate. If you are selling stocks you have owned for less than a year, you will pay your highest marginal rate. You can also seek out investments that are tax sensitive (there are many investments available that either have low turnover and/or manage their funds to be tax efficient), tax-advantage (for example many municipal bonds are federal tax free, but some are subject to

"AMT" or alternative minimum tax so be sure to do your homework on these).

Today is the day to plan your strategy for future tax planning.  If you do your own taxes make a goal for a consultation, just to make sure you are on track.  If you work with tax and financial professionals, make sure you are doing all you can to minimize your tax bite.  Some of the following tax planning opportunities may apply, or your goal may be as simple as consulting a tax professional for their guidance.  If you are not sure if the best place to save is your 401k or a Roth IRA, or what particular items to invest in based on whether an account is taxable or not, add more specific considerations to the goal list that follows and plan a date to finish and or understand  them by:

To fulfill this goal I need to take each of these steps, one at a time:

1. _____ by: _____

3. _____ by: _____

3. _____ by: _____

# Retirement Planning 101

# Day 19

## Retirement Plans

*"Life is full of uncertainties. Future investment earnings and interest and inflation rates are not known to anybody. However, I can guarantee you one thing...those who put an investment program in place will have a lot more money when they come to retire than those who never get around to it."*
*~Noel Whittaker*

One of my favorite clients asked me to sit down with her college age niece and explain the investment and financial planning world. My client and I were thrilled at the chance to meet with a 21-year-old who wanted to meet with us and discuss how the world of money worked. Why were we so darn excited? We wished someone had sat us down at an early age and explained what a marvelous opportunity we had right in front of us. We now know that the earlier you begin to put money away the quicker it accumulates. My client created a spreadsheet showing how her little IRA contribution had grown over the years into an exceptional nest egg.

This section will quickly touch on the types of retirement accounts you may have available to allocate your spending plan amounts to and suggestions for how to use them to your best advantage.

If your employer offers a 401(k), 403(b) or a 457 plan these are typically a way for your company to contribute funds to your retirement and an avenue for you to put away a significant amount of before-tax money each year that can then grow tax deferred. Be aware of how much your company contributes and whether that amount is dependent on how much you put into your plan. Do not overlook this, as it is essentially "free" money that is being offered to you as a match to what you put in. Getting this "match" should be one of your top saving priorities. These types of plans can usually move to new jobs, or be "rolled over" into a rollover IRA and it is wise to keep your retirement plan consolidated in a central location--the better to look after it. Some of these plans also offer the ability to take loans against a portion of your balance. Besides being one of the quickest ways to put a large dent in your retirement plan, if you are doing your spending allocation wisely, you will have allocated a portion of your assets to an emergency account, hopefully removing the need for a loan--ever.

If you find yourself with a small retirement plan from a former employer, resist any temptation to cash it out, as you pay a 10 percent penalty, plus your ordinary income tax on the entire amount. Instead of relying on the government or a pension to plan your retirement for you, you have the chance to manage it yourself, so pay attention to every little penny and make good decisions to keep the account intact and growing.

Pension plans, defined benefit plans and defined contribution plans are not as common these days, but if they are available, be sure to understand your contributions (if any), your employer's contribution, and any vesting and or employee match rules.

Individual Retirement Accounts or "IRAs" are another way to stash away pre-tax income and grow it without taxation, until you take withdrawals. The maximum contributions change each year, and there may be limitations based on your income. If you qualify, it is another potential way to sock away some funds.

Roth IRAs are different in that you contribute money, after taxes, thus you do not get an immediate tax savings to contribute. However, the tax savings can be huge when you do not have to pay taxes *ever* during your withdrawal period in retirement. There are varying income limitations for these unique savings vehicles, and you can definitely gain in using these as another way to diversify your source of income funds during retirement.

Both IRAs and Roth IRAs offer impressive benefits for first time homebuyers as well.

If you own a business, there are a myriad of retirement plans you can use to not only benefit yourself and your family, but also any employees you have. These plans could allow you to put away far more than traditional 401K-based plans so do not overlook them.

A traditional investment account is a savings account with your post tax dollars that will usually be taxed at the capital gains rate. At this time, that is lower than your ordinary income tax rate, so another good way to contribute to something slightly different so you don't end up with all of your withdrawal eggs from the same tax basket.

Check with your accountant and your financial advisor to be sure you are taking advantage of every tax-advantaged savings approach you can. Any of these accounts can be invested in stocks, bonds, mutual funds, fixed income funds, annuities and company stock or a mix of any of these. Some plans allow you to buy your own employer's stock.

Make sure you are maximizing your retirement contributions today and understanding your employer plans by:

1. What is the maximum amount of money I can be putting into a retirement plan right now? $_____

2. Does my employer match? _____

3. How much can I (or we) put into a retirement plan each year? $_____

# Day 20

## How Much Do You Need?

*"Money is the opposite of the weather. Nobody talks about it,*
*but everybody does something about it."*
*~ Rebecca Johnson*

There is an advertisement running on TV right now that shows people walking to work or playing, but all holding a set of numbers about five feet long. Each person carries a different amount, but these numbers all seem to be an onerous burden to fit onto elevators, into the car and carry about one's daily business. The commercial is about figuring out how much you need to retire on and planning for that amount. I think it is a subtle symbol for the shadow of worry that many of us carry around in our normal lives, wondering, "Do I have enough to retire on?"

Karen and Bob asked to meet with me to discuss their investment planning. As we were going through the discovery process it became apparent that there were some unresolved money issues between them, yet it was not clear as to what or why. From my outside perspective I was able to see that they had good money habits, and had the potential to easily alter their spending targets so they could have enough to retire on. However, before we had that discussion, I had the occasion to speak to each of them privately. They each wanted me to know that the other spouse had a spending or lack of saving problem and they were terrified about impending retirement issues. I realized they had let "the number" become an unspoken burden between them, causing untold arguments that were not really about the issue at hand but were just two people who loved each other deeply, but were scared that they were never going to have enough to choose how they spent their remaining years on earth. Once we finished the income planning process and goals, and had some defined spending targets to invest in, Karen and Bob couldn't believe the change in their relationship. They ended up doubling their savings goals and have had the luxury of changing their lifestyles to do things they loved.

You have done all of this work, gathering financial information, getting clear about your spending plan and recording your goals. Many of us have a murky idea of what will happen when we no longer have our salary-based income. We imagine that the amounts we're setting aside in our retirement plans, pensions or savings as well as what we have coming from social security and Medicare are all going to coalesce together into our "retirement income." For many individuals and couples there is a complete avoidance of the discussion.

This type of shadow fear can influence every part of our lives--single or married--and chip away at our commitment to make phenomenal spending plans and stick to them. Go through this process, preferably with a Certified Financial Planner™. I will outline some general guidelines as to how much you need, but the services of an objective consultant will be worth your investment.

Your retirement income will be based on your assets, any pensions, Social Security and any other income that will flow to you. The rule of thumb is to estimate that your investible assets (not your home, but monies that are growing and generating annual income) will supply approximately 4% income of your asset balance. That means if you have an account with $500,000 in it, you can usually safely withdraw $20,000 a year in income.

Take your Social Security estimate (if you do not have your annual statement available you can obtain an estimate at www.ssa.gov), and add in pensions and other income:

Amount of investments:

$_____ times 4% = $_____ per year

Social Security estimate:        $_____ per year

Pension / Annuity:               $_____ per year

Rental Income:                   $_____ per year

Other Income:                    $_____ per year

Grand Total Income Estimate: $_____ per year

While this is a somewhat simplistic analysis, it's designed to get you started on the path to retirement income planning.  If you are not sure how much you will actually need to live on, plan on 70 to 75 percent of your pre-retirement income to have the same level of comfort.  There are many vital mitigating factors to consider when doing this type of analysis like inflation, incomes that may not keep up with inflation, asset returns and potential health care costs, so take the time to do this analysis with an experienced financial planner.

If you happen to feel mildly terrified at the prospect of generating enough income to live on, remember that your true "number" may not be the rote definition of a percentage of your current income, or the concept of retirement as promulgated by the media (golf/cruises/vacation home, etc). There are two hugely significant variables here. One, by going through this exercise it will give you clarity as to where you should be investing your spending plan amounts. That in itself can have powerful consequences for your asset level.

The second, and most important, is that you define the specific nuances of how you retire. Perhaps going through this creates one of those "aha" moments where, after you have recovered from the fact that your income will be $30,000 short per year, you realize that you could retire from a job you don't care for and then work at a job you love and "only" have to generate that income to continue your standard of living. Downsizing real estate can add another chunk into your nest egg or relocating to an area that costs less to live. If you don't have to commute to a job, but take a part-time job near your home, you may have decreased your commuter costs, and still find yourself generating another slice of the pie to your income.

Other areas of your retirement that only you will define are coaching yourself to be flexible about when you spend money. If you plan to take 4 percent a year in income from your investments, while knowing that in good years you may be able to take extra, but in bad years you will skip the extra income, that concept can be a helpful buffer to prevent your portfolio from drawing down too soon. You may plan to spend more when you are in your sixties than when you are older, and structure your spend-down accordingly.

Most importantly, just like creating a "spending plan" instead of a "mandatory budget," living simply during retirement isn't just about resentfully denying yourself the pleasures of life. It is about thoughtfully deciding what truly fulfills you and then building a life you love based on what will be your greatest freedom--time and flexibility to choose how to spend it.

# Day 21

# What if You Don't Have Enough?

*"Lack of money is no obstacle. Lack of an idea is an obstacle."*
*~Hakuta, Ken*

If you have just finished the last section, and are disheartened with the realization that it seems that you absolutely don't have enough, this chapter is for you. I've read a plethora of money self help books, articles and advice and often I find the happy, "here is how it's all going to work" section and I wonder what someone does if they can't see the light at the end of the tunnel.

Well, here we are. I'm not one for sugarcoating and wish that every financial guide would be this straightforward. If you haven't got enough, then you need to creatively and radically modify your life, your standard of living and your assumptions of your future. Even unhappier than retirees who don't have enough money are retirees who expected to have money, and ended up with next to nothing. It is those expectations that can have a vital role in our state of happiness. We've already discussed some different approaches to one's attitude toward a spending plan and outlining what is truly important (which you may have noticed has very little to do with money).

Another note I'll make about this chapter is that although it may not apply directly to you, or you may wonder how you ever got yourself in this spot in the first place. Life is funny in that the trajectory we end up taking may not be consistent with where we thought we would end up. I remember a time in my life when I had gotten off course financially. I was sharing my woes with a long time financial advisor who had seen her share of life's ups and downs. As I was lamenting, she began suggesting several very viable changes to my life that would solve my financial issues and give me the leverage I needed to change my future. At first I was embarrassed at the perceived step down my life would have to take (smaller home, etc.) and then I was aghast at the thought of having to change my life. You see, the truly terrifying thing was that I might have to *change* my habits, my expectations and my comfortable routine. She was so right, and really the only one with the courage to tell me the unwelcome truth. So let me bring that gift to you.

This chapter is about triage. The three areas of financial emergency that must be attended to if you have the sinking suspicion that you are severely off track financially and you truly want to realize the life you intend.

What is your current standard of living? Be tough on yourself here knowing that you have developed some critical skills while working through this book in the area of knowing your assets, your spending plan and your goals. If this is depressing to you, or you feel that life has handed the "unexpected" and you want to avoid dealing with it, my heartfelt advice is to instead take it for what it is--a masterful learning experience that will grow you into a stronger person. I challenge you to think from of a place of power and control (not fear) of what you do to change your life.

<u>Triage One</u>: Your Life – current standard of living – how much do I think I need vs. actual expenses?

_____

_____

_____

<u>Triage Two</u>: Income – is there a way to bring in more, or to supplement my income?

_____

_____

_____

<u>Triage Three</u>: How could my expectations change?

_____

_____

_____

What if that is not enough to live on? Some other ways to change the way I make assumptions about my retirement income are:

1. _____

2. _____

3. _____

# Day 22

# Will it Last?

*"Retirement is like a long vacation in Las Vegas. The goal is to enjoy it the fullest,*
*but not so fully that you run out of money."*
*~Jonathan Clements*

In a 2005 "USA Today" poll, running out of money was not listed as the top concern for those facing aging and retirement[1]. In fact, it wasn't even second or third. Running out of money came in a distant fourth, and was a lower concern for those with the highest incomes. The three items that came in higher were health or quality of health issues. After that, what was the number one fear? Money, money, and money. About the same time, the Census Bureau estimated that by 2050 more than a million Americans will be over 100 years old. Studies right and left have been showing that not only are we living longer, but also we're healthier longer. All good, but it comes back to that little concern, how are we going to make it last?

Just like the last section, the greatest service I can give my readers is to frankly discuss the implications of planning for your nest egg to last thirty, forty or even fifty years. Previous generations did not

---

[1] http://abcnews.go.com/images/Politics/995a1Longevity.pdf

have the same circumstances that we are experiencing today. The average lifespan was less and many employers offered life-long pension plans to provide income to retirees. Social Security was originally designed to offer an income during the last *few* years of life, not provide an income for decades, just as Medicare and Medicaid have been burdened further than their intended use. Flash forward to today and most employers are ditching life-long pension plans like hot potatoes. Warnings about rapidly inflating health care costs, long term care, and the constant hum of politicos and the media about the unhealthy state of the U.S. entitlement programs (Social Security, Medicare and Medicaid) are enough to give us pessimistic thoughts of our future lives here on earth. While it is entirely likely that SSA benefits will not be as big a part of our income as we had expected, or that government medical benefits are going to become tighter, let's not let that stop us from planning and enjoying the gift of a long lifetime.

Your first objective is to plan to maximize your income earning years to your advantage, while enjoying the heck out of your present life. Your second objective is to do a fantastic job of managing your assets not only until you retire, but also after you retire with a realistic viewpoint on what happens when things don't go as we expected, and what to do about it. Take control of your future today, plan for inventive self-reliance in your future and do not let all of the potential "what-ifs" interfere any longer with the present.

Objective one is to, in the here and now, (no matter how far from, or how close you are to retirement), direct your spending plan to include an allocation to your "giving up work time line," your savings, or your legacy goals that need to be supported financially. Because by doing this you are fulfilling one of your top three legacy goals, in one way or another this should be a short list of focused efforts. When you concentrate on something single-mindedly, it will get done.

While being mindful of the fact that our true enjoyment should be centered in the immediate and the present, living and experiencing our lives, the art of living is to be able to find fulfillment each day, while also investing in your future legacy. This may mean living a simple life now, planning to generate income longer or strategizing on ways to generate additional income. This is not about sacrificing the present for the future, but about living life with imagination and purpose. When considering your future, remember that it will always be a far easier choice to choose working a few additional years, or reducing to part-time work, than it is to go out and look for a new job when you are in your sixties and above

An acquaintance of mine works for a non-profit group that helps very ill people find healthy organs. His job is to travel quickly to hospitals across the northwest, and collect the heart or other vital parts of some forward-thinking soul who marked "Organ Donor" on a driver's license. I asked him what it was like, racing to the bedside of an otherwise healthy individual, knowing he was only there to remove parts of someone's brain-dead body. His answer changed my perspective on everything I do and how I live. He said, as he "meets" the person, who just that morning woke up, had a to-do list and ran the errands of family and work, he stops to remember that an awareness of our mortality is the greatest gift in the world. Each healthy body he meets reminds him that we have no idea how long our clock will tick. This section is essentially about the risk that your clock will tick a lot longer than you realize. While aggressively planning for that, wake up each morning determined to make the most of your job, your relationships, and your awareness for the beautiful world around us. That may mean taking your kids on camping trips instead of a resort in a warm place; it may mean driving a car a few years older than brand new or cooking great food at home instead of going out to eat. What it does NOT mean is a mentality of denial. It is about creating a life or a job that is so enjoyable it may continue to be a part of your life for years past the "official" retirement age. As your financial planner, it could be defined as another income source. But, as a human, in order to arrive at that kind of imaginative living, you must realize that the every day of life is a state of mind that you choose.

Objective two is the art of managing your assets for now, for the future and for the unexpected.  Sounds like a tall order, but with understanding and planning, it can be a series of simple techniques and decisions that add up to a smart label on you a few decades later.  Most likely you have a 401K, or other self-directed retirement plan (meaning not a pension) at your disposal.  Even if you have a pension, don't let that stop you from maximizing other retirement plans.  Pensions are not fool proof, just ask the former employees of now defunct airlines or manufacturing companies.

Your mission is to have a diversified basket from which you will save and then draw income from, and if a portion of that is some sort of pension income, then that's excellent, add it to the list.  If, like the majority of Americans, you just have traditional retirement plans available, try to take advantage of everything you can.  Max out your 401K (especially making sure you are contributing enough to receive a matching contribution from your employer), contribute to IRAs, Roth IRAs, Health Savings Accounts, and Education plans if you qualify, and if you have the funds.  Plan your investments to grow steadily, without taking any outsize risks.  More specific investment guidelines will be discussed later on.  But it's worth noting now, that one problem of self directed retirement plans is that some contributors take too much risk, others not enough and both end up negating the future growth they so vitally need.

Remember the fable about the tortoise and the hare?  Thoughtfully allocating your resources not only to different types of tax advantaged accounts, but in some cases, different types of investments can be another way to hedge yourself from the unexpected.  As you are so diligently saving and allocating to different types of plans, some tax-favored, some not, you are slowly but steadily creating several baskets of assets that have different taxation and growth advantages.

In addition to the "problem" of not knowing how long you are going to live, there is another issue of timing. You may be asking, just how many issues can there be with living a long and healthy life? Well, let's say you've diligently saved and diversified your portfolio for the last four decades or so, and the year that you decide to retire, the stock market goes through the greatest bear market of all time. Your tidy little nest egg just took a hit from which it may take another decade to recover, and suddenly, your "number" has changed. Don't discount these new variations on ways to plan for the future, but don't enter into them without the guidance of your tax and financial professional and an eyes wide-open perspective. The key is to not put your eggs all in one basket. There are so many unknowns for us healthy, long-living citizens who can't predict when a massive dip in the market may occur, that balancing your assets in different areas can be just what the retirement doctor ordered.

Today I will make sure I am maximizing and diversify my spending targets to saving for my legacy goals. I will examine my plan and see how much I can be contributing to retirement plans and savings, research other assets to diversify into and consider how to generate income from something I love.

Today I will answer these questions:

1. What is the 4% theory?
2. Am I diversified in both income and investments?
3. Am I willing to be flexible if things don't go as expected?

# Investing 101

# Day 23

# The Basics

*"Rednecks think mutual funds means
everybody's having a good time."*
~ Jeff Foxworthy

In the year 1999, I felt rich, rich, rich! Every month when my investment statement came in the mail, I would spend the next few weeks dreaming of the life of leisure that was sure to be mine, with my money growing by 20 to 40 percent a year. Yahoo! I loved Microsoft, Intel and Infospace too! When things started heading the other way in March of 2000, I stopped celebrating and started thinking. Wasn't this investing business just an erratic business of incomprehensible formulas, odd jargon and pure luck? I felt like I had been playing a game and it had all been a matter of chance. Many people and clients I have spoken with throughout the years have relayed the same feelings to me. Have you ever felt like you didn't want to trust your hard earned money to an investment world that you not only felt you had no control of but didn't understand either? If so, this chapter is for you.

All of the above perceptions are quite ordinary, but they are oh so wrong. Becoming a successful investor has nothing to do with luck, accidents or those magic investment formulas touted on the Internet and TV. You don't have to be a genius or MIT graduate to win, although it can be nice to have those sorts of professionals managing your money for you!  The world of stocks and investments is not only far from a game, but it is about the economy, both locally and globally, that we are each a member of. Like it or not, it is part of each of our collective trip through life on spaceship earth.  If you want to arrive at a specific location, take the time now to understand how to get there and what the ride will be like.  That will give you the advance guidance you will need to make decisions when the journey seems rocky.

I have run into a couple of distinctive roadblocks that some people use to avoid learning about or understanding investing in their future.  On one hand some assume that the "government" or their company will take care of that planning for them.  Around retirement age, income will continue to flow their way, just like it did for their parents or grandparents.  On the other hand are those that are so overwhelmed they either disagree with the concept that investing is risky or a gamble, or refuse to learn about it and mindlessly let someone else or an institution manage their hard earned assets for them, with no personal oversight.  Both of these approaches are an excuse.  This is the time to ask yourself, "How much do I want my legacy goals?"  If you truly desire and want them bad enough, you must take the time to understand the basic framework of how money and investing works.  If you want to arrive at your ultimate legacy goal, realize now that counting on some antiquated viewpoint of a paternal government or institution to hand us our dreams on a silver platter is never going to happen. Although that might have worked for a couple of generations in our country's history, the social security and pension pyramid is not guaranteed to benefit us in the same way.  That does not mean you need to be in charge of your money yourself.  It is an enhancement to work with professionals to guide you along the way.  However, it does mean you take responsibility for understanding the foundation upon which your financial home is built.  Doing so will give you the framework you need to accurately determine if you are on track and to evaluate your choices.  It will also give you the ability to master your subjective feelings of fear and greed, so your choices will come from sound long-term planning instead.

First off, why do we have to invest, can't we just save our money and earn a little interest on the way? Sounds safe, but if you got a statement every month in the mail showing how much your dollars were now worth after inflation was subtracted out, you would suddenly see in black and white how much you lose by not keeping up with inflation. Historically, inflation has averaged more than 3 percent for the last century or so. That means that if you have $1,000 today, in twenty years it will be worth $500 in spending power. Another reason to invest in retirement plans that are tax deferred is a thoughtful benefit extended to us by our government. It is the chance to earn deferred growth on their money (well, money they would have collected in taxes) for decades. As noted in the last chapter, you can avoid paying taxes (the average is around 20 to 25 percent) now and let your account grow tax-free until you take withdrawals from the account in your retirement years. It is yet another reason to take control of our own retirement planning instead of assuming (hoping) that someone else will do it.

Now is the time during the investment planning part of our relationship that a client may ask me, "Is there any chance I could lose everything?" The SEC and other protectors of financial consumers have made the printed and stated phrase, "past performance is no guarantee of future success" ubiquitous in any financial literature or presentations. There is a reason for that, and it is vital to understand why. Many people don't take the time to understand investments and end up losing a lot of money. The reason you are taking the time to read this guide and oversee your financial future is so that does not happen to you. Investing is always a risk, as well as inflation, interest rates, currency changes and market volatility. The only way to manage all of these risks with the intent of growing your portfolio over time is to understand the risks. Market volatility means that those investments you make in your 401K in mutual funds, or that stock you buy may go up or down in value in the short term. There are no promises that your investment will go up. However, something I have banked on my entire life is "probabilities." While I cannot predict what will happen in the short term, in the investment world, with companies and with the economy (okay, and often with my own life too), I can say that most likely, our country will continue to provide economic growth and freedom to its citizens. If I continue to save and diversify among several of these companies, in the long term and on average, my portfolio will grow. In order to stay focused on probabilities, one needs to understand the concept of "time." To those terrified of the daily, monthly and sometimes yearly fluctuations of the stock market I would advise them to look at any long-term (more than ten year) charts of investment performance. History shows that if you can stick to a long-term plan, it will pay off over time. During volatility, recessions, political instability and wars the stock market has earned an average, annualized 10 percent rate of return per year. Remember that this discussion is about long term investing to reach long-standing goals. If you have some short-term legacy goals to reach in the next three to ten years, focus on saving, not investing.

Today you will examine if your investment decisions have been driven by paralysis, fear or greed and consider your true perspective towards investing (gambling, luck or thoughtful approach). Look at your past choices and read on for more direction in the roadmap of your financial life. Be clear on your time horizons:

| 1. Copy Your Legacy Goals | 2. Assign Your Time Horizons |
|---|---|
|  |  |
|  |  |
|  |  |

3. Ensure that your investments are properly aligned with your goals by checking them yourself, and/or communicating with your financial advisor.

# Day 24

## Compound Growth

*"The most powerful force in the universe is compound interest"*
*~Albert Einstein*

One of the great thinkers of the world, Albert Einstein, took time from his busy schedule of inventing and articulating profound theories to acknowledge the magic and power of compounding growth.  It is a simple concept that we all learn in grade school, but it is easily forgotten, especially if you feel like you may be starting later in life to save.  Do not fear, compound growth works at any age, and is a marvelous idea to keep in mind.

The more time you have to invest, the more powerful compound growth is to your future.  Compounding simply means that the investments or savings you earmark to earn an annual rate of return (over time) begin to build on themselves.  The interest (or rate of return) is added to the original amount and then the total of principal plus interest earns even more interest.  Remember the brainteaser about the penny? Would you rather have $1,000 today, or only one penny, but with the guarantee that the penny would double in value every day for a month?  One thousand dollars sounds nice, I'll take it.  However, if one examines the growth of the penny, one will find it worth over a million dollars a month later.  While I won't recommend an investment that routinely doubles in value, like the theoretical penny in this brainteaser (there's that whole risk thing), even an investment that grows at a conservative rate of return of around 7 percent will double in value in ten years. A quick approach to determining how fast your nest egg will double in value was also made famous by Einstein, "The Rule of 72." Just take the number "72" and divide it by your annual rate of return. Thus 72 divided by 7 percent equals 10.2 years.

The most important impression that I want to make with this section is that along with the "magic" of compound growth, is the fact that the earlier you start the better. It is never too late, and if you are putting off saving for the future because it seems to have less impact at your current age, do not ever buy into that mode of thought. Most of the glamorous examples of compound growth will show an example of one 20-year-old who put away x amount of dollars for ten years, and then never put away another penny, then another 20-year-old who waited until he was in his thirties to put away ten times more money on a yearly basis. At the age of 65, the early bird has more money and had to save ten times less, while the late bloomer has less money and had to save more. Very impressive, but these famous examples don't acknowledge that your time may be right now. Perhaps you are in your later years, but the numerical growth is the same, and, guess what?, you may just live a lot longer than you realize, so although you may not be a twenty-something, your time horizon still fits on these charts.

The last point on compound growth I want to leave with you is that you've just been appointed as an "Einstein Evangelist." Adhering to and teaching the benefits of saving and growing your money can be an amazing gift to share with the young people in our lives. Either by example or communication show what can happen if one begins early and routinely invests over time. Today is a good day to look back on your investments and realize how much they have grown over time, or to plan ahead for your future growth that will come from sticking to a long-term plan. If the idea of diverting money into a savings plan sounds challenging in light of all of the other things you would like to purchase or consume, then ask yourself, "How bad do I want it?"

1. How much is a $250.00 pair of shoes worth in 20 years? _____

2. How much is $250.00 in an IRA worth in 20 years? _____

3. How much is a $30,000 car worth in five years? _____

4. How much is $500.00 invested monthly at 8% growth worth in five years? _____

(Answers)
1. Subjective amount, but generally not much!
2. About $1165.00 at an 8% annual growth rate.
3. Subjective amount, but around $10,000
4. About **$298,000** at an 8% annual growth rate.

# Day 25

## Where to Invest and How to Know What to Invest in?

*"Money is like manure. You have to spread it around or it smells."*
*~J. Paul Getty*

I knew something was going on this year when I noticed more than the usual slew of investment commercials, complete with memory-tugging classics of the seventies humming along in the background, with gray-haired once-famous people talking about where and how to invest money. Then, it was the first official baby boomer, born one second after midnight in January 1946, arriving to collect her first social security check. Ah, the demographic had arrived, along with their retirement plans! These days more than ever, it seems there are a thousand alleged wonderful places and ideas of where to invest your nest egg. Despite the obvious idea of engaging a professional financial planner to help guide you, let's take a look at the myriad of choices out there and keep things simple.

David Swensen leads the $22.5 **billion** endowment at Yale investment management team. With all of the complex and intricate investment strategies he has used to make this fund successful, you would think him to be an excellent advisor.

Surprisingly, in his book, "Unconventional Success: A Fundamental Approach to Personal Investment," he suggests a portfolio that essentially has five types of investments using index funds or exchange traded funds. "Wait a minute!" an excited investor said to me a few months ago. "What about that hot stock I saw on a TV show last week, and then that other company that I know a lot about because I'm a customer?" The truth is, just like the Getty quote above, it is vital to spread your money around. Buying single stocks or investing in hot sectors just does not work for the average investor. Most people do not have the resources, time and knowledge to choose the best stocks or other individual investments, and then apply a disciplined approach to when to sell and buy. A few years ago, a well-known research firm published a study on individual investment performance with startling results. During a twenty-year period in which the S&P 500 returned 11.9 percent, the average investor earned 3.7 percent. It seems that investors were routinely moving into funds that had recently had high returns, and moving out of funds that had low returns[2]. As David Swensen points out, investors, just like many financial professionals already do, need to follow a long-term, prudent plan in order to realize success and not try to maximize returns on high-risk investments, or fail to protect their portfolio by diversifying.

In the spirit of keeping it simple, let's review how simple investment asset allocation can be. There are essentially three types of things to invest your money in: stocks, bonds and cash. (Not included in this discussion are the more philosophical concepts of investing in yourself, your business or real estate.)

Stocks work like this: a company will issue stock for sale and use the money raised to grow its business. The buyer of the stock then owns a portion of the company and has the ability to vote on decisions that influence the company. New investors can purchase shares of an existing company from other shareholders when they

---

[2]http://www.dalbar.com

believe the value of the stock will go up, and/or to receive dividends that a company may pay its stockholders.

Bonds work like this: a company or the government will take a loan from investors. The loan proceeds are used to fund growth for the business, or in the case of governments, to build things that benefit taxpayers like schools and roads. The investor consents to loan money to an entity in return for getting paid interest on the loan and a promise that the amount loaned will be returned in full on a particular date. Some existing bonds (loans) can then be sold to other investors much like stocks can, although the sale price could be higher or lower than the purchase value of the bond. Regardless of the fluctuating sale value of the bond, it does not affect the interest paid and due date value of the bond. The investor that buys an ongoing bond on the market can then receive the interest and return of principal based on the original terms of the "loan."

Cash works like this: a financial institution, typically insured by the federal government through FDIC insurance, will offer investors a rate of return on funds that the investors place into accounts held at the bank. The rate may fluctuate on a daily basis, depending on the interest rate environment. The investor has access to the cash at any time, and the amount deposited does not fluctuate in value and is readily available to the investor.

A plethora of products to invest in is lobbed to every consumer each day. It can seem overwhelming and even intimidating to choose what to invest in. Today we will take a look at what it means to invest in these three assets, and in the next chapter will guide you on how to design a plan that will clarify where each of your dollars should be invested, no matter what happens in the financial world.

For most people, equities (stocks) have become a common item for either them, or their retirement plan, to use in their allocations in order to grow, keep up with inflation and provide for future income. As more and more of us have become primarily responsible for making the choices, looking at the headlines can profoundly influence our opinion of whether it is a good time, or even a legitimate idea to invest in stocks. When one is afflicted by financial hypochondria, it is helpful to take a look at history. During and right after the energy crisis of the 70's, the stock market crash of 1987, the Persian Gulf War in 1991 or the 9-11 attack on the World Trade Center, it seemed like a terrible time to invest in stocks. However if one looks at the valuations of stocks and traces the upward trajectory in value from the seventies until current day, anyone who implemented a diversified plan made positive returns, over the long term, despite the ebbs and flows of the economic times or news.

Notice the use of the phrase, "diversified plan" in the above sentence. The secret to investing without all of the volatility is to just spread things around. A more official phrase would be asset allocation. That means that just as you should place differing percentages of your money in stocks, bonds and cash, you should also place differing percentages into different types of stocks. Again, there is the potential for too much information, as there are literally thousands of ways (and advertisements) as to how to invest in different types of stocks. Back to keeping it simple...there are essentially nine types of stocks you can allocate into.

The easiest way to keep it straight is the common "tic tac toe" board used in many financial analyses (Asset allocation cannot eliminate the risk of fluctuating prices and uncertain returns.):

| Large Size Value Companies | Large Size Core Companies | Large Size Growth Companies |
|---|---|---|
| Mid Size Value Companies | Mid Size Core Companies | Mid Size Growth Companies |
| Small Size Value Companies | Small Size Core Companies | Small Size Growth Companies |

Investing is simple when one realizes that you only need to first insure that you have evaluated your risk and time horizon in order to intelligently allocate differing amounts to stocks, bonds and cash and then create a plan for how much of your stock funds will be allocated to the "tick tack toe" board of the nine types of investments. While one does not need a myriad of complex investment ideas at this point, it is important to not underestimate the support of a financial advisor to guide in allocation choices (for example the nuances between your exposure to international and emerging markets, commodities or even real estate) and to accurately and objectively evaluate risk and time parameters.

While we have boiled down investing in stocks to a simplistic look at nine areas, it is important to remember that stocks are not pledged to earning the investor more money. In fact, even sound companies can lose stock value, and some stocks can completely lose any value. The best way to avoid exposure to single company risk is to make sure that a portfolio is diversified among each of the nine sectors.

Today I will look at my investments and ask:

1. Have I created a plan that reflects my short and long term financial goals and then structured my investments accordingly?
2. Am I exposed to just a few companies or sectors, or is my portfolio diversified?
3. Have I consulted with an advisor as a "check up" to make sure that my risk profile and time horizon are accurately reflected in my investments?

# Day 26

# Before You Ever Invest a Penny, Invest in an "Investment Policy Statement"

*"Invest a few moments in thinking. It will pay good interest."*
*~Author Unknown*

One sunny summer day in a neighboring state, I was driving my blended family of six back to the hotel from a wonderfully exhausting day at the amusement park. Marrying a man who often got lost and never asked for directions had emboldened my perception of my own spotty, but still sometimes uncanny, geographical abilities. Consequently, when he inquired as to whether I knew where I was going, I flippantly asked him if he was daring to question my superior directionality. When the five minute trip had turned into twenty and the peanut gallery a couple of rows back was making quips about mom's "directionality," I refused to admit that something had gone terribly wrong in the driver's seat and even drove on for another few miles trying to reconcile the lack of a hotel appearing on the horizon with the vast swaths of forest that were growing before my eyes. In retrospect, and after the ensuing teasing I've endured from loved ones who weren't even in the car that day, I've realized that I was merely a prime example of the biggest mistake an investor can make in managing their portfolio--lack of a road map.

An Investment Policy Statement is just that, a road map. It articulates where you are today, where you want to be in the future and how you will get there. It gives a guide to the boundaries of how, when and why your dollars will be invested over time. A road map allows the driver to not be intimidated by unknown terrain, confusing road signs or other drivers. It gives the driver the confidence to enjoy the trip, knowing that many unexpected twists and turns have been accounted for already.

Successful endowments, pension and money managers all use Investment Policy Statements. A few years ago some forward thinking financial advisors and planners began to help clients create their own personalized IPS plans and then use these as guides to help manage their portfolios. This takes any guessing out of your investments and helps one stick to a long term plan of diversification and re-balancing a portfolio when different asset classes grow beyond the parameters of sound diversification. The results can be powerful when one is able to look at a plan or roadmap on paper and know that although the stock market looks downright scary and the media is selling fear, none of that matters because the IPS is designed for a twenty or thirty year plan and time specific goals, not a sound bite time horizon.

Completing an investment plan will furnish the magic "number" that one needs to meet legacy goals such as retirement at a certain income, a particular age or whatever else is on that heartfelt list. The investment plan also shows what annualized rate of return one needs to arrive at that goal, and even how many additional dollars one needs to put aside to achieve their ambitions. Armed with that information, an IPS will outline where your current assets are, what types of accounts they are held in (important for strategic tax planning) and how much money you intend to put away. It will list your upcoming short-term cash flow needs and wishes, your medium-term aims to reach and your long-term retirement targets and other intentions for that time period. It will then decipher what assets should be placed in cash, bonds or stocks in order to meet those goals, and how your assets should be invested, not only among the three big classes of investment, but of the nine style boxes of stocks in order to meet your desired rate of return (over time of course) with the least amount of risk possible. It also is an excellent way to analyze tax implications of where certain types of investments are placed and model what happens if things don't go as expected. This provides oversight in the long term as you have a document to look back on and remember why particular choices were made. It is your own personal checks and balances system. For example, if one just read that Costco is rationing rice, commodities are making a ton of money, and selling out the bond portfolio and investing in grain futures suddenly seems like an excellent detour to take; things may seem a little different when the road map is pulled out and consulted!

Anecdotally, I have found that when there is more than one person involved in the outcome to a financial plan, as in most marriages and partnerships, having a plan to refer to can defuse arguments and give guidance when making important decisions.

Ah, what a relief to know that although the sky is falling in and Chicken Little is interviewing a famous economist on CNN, one's Investment Policy Statement is chugging along in a disciplined, unemotional manner working for you while you sleep at night.

Today I will call my CFP® or my financial advisor and discuss an Investment Policy Statement.

For my Investment Policy Statement:

1.    How long until I retire or need income?
2.    What percentage will go into stocks, bonds and cash?
3.    Do my investments fit with my legacy goals?

# Day 27

# Don't Rely on Your Brain or Gut to Make Financial Decisions

*"We simply attempt to be fearful when others are greedy and to be greedy only when others are fearful."*
*~Warren Buffett*

A recent research project gave unusual insight into how our amazing brains work. In the test, researchers flashed two lights (one red and one green) completely haphazardly, on a screen. However there was one catch, the green light flashed 80 percent of the time and the red light only 20 percent. In repeated tests, across the human spectrum, our fellow citizens consistently attempted to guess when the red light would flash. That means that instead of choosing to pick green all of the time, and then having an eighty percent accuracy rating, their guesses on when the red would occur lowered their results to, on average, 68 percent. The twist in the experiment is that when rats and pigeons receive food for the right choice they quickly learn to choose green every time, thus giving them an 80 percent accuracy rating!

This test, like many others that measure the consistency of our irrational brains, have been around for years and were recently compiled into a brilliant book that we all ought to read on an annual basis. "Your Money & Your Brain," by Jason Zweig, explores the facts behind the link between emotional decision-making when it comes to our hard earned coins. Zweig notes, "Economists have long insisted that investors use information logically. In practice, however, those assumptions often turn out to be dead wrong." Included in the book are these key observations:

- A monetary loss or gain is not just a financial or psychological outcome but also a biological change that has profound physical effects on the brain and body.
- The neural activity of someone whose investments are climbing is no different from that of someone high on cocaine or morphine.
- Financial losses are processed in the same areas of the brain that respond to mortal danger.

These inherent irrationalities that exist in the gray matter between our ears must be acknowledged and addressed, or it will affect our decision-making at the worst possible time. The first step is for each one of us to take ownership of our financial lives and take the time to create a plan that outlines not only how much is enough, but how much risk we will take with our finances. Knowledge is power, and just as we are taking the time to understand how we cannot just trust our instincts or brain to guide us, we can also see that if we take the time to understand the basic principals of saving and investing we'll have the power to make great decisions.

Human psychology is the bedrock of why we do the things we do, and understanding that can be the key to protecting our portfolio from ourselves. Have you ever made a mistake and just hated to admit it? (I am flashbacking to my infamous drive to nowhere on my family vacation. It took me twenty minutes to reverse course even though it was quickly obvious I had made a colossal misjudgment.) Acknowledging and apologizing for something can be a challenging experience for anybody. The same human behavior applies to our money decisions, and based on the research above, may be even more pronounced. People hate to admit making a mistake, particularly when it's a bad investment. As a result, they tend to irrationally hold on to losing choices, because if they sell them it will make the loss, or mistake, official. Other times, when they've made a great investment they will sell it too early in order to realize the win or the gain. This illogical behavior has actually been studied in great detail and was part of a Nobel Prize winner's research in behavioral finance. To escape from the cycle of poor financial decisions here are three simple tenants to follow:

1. Don't use the past to make future decisions. Just ask anyone who swarmed into hot technology and Internet ideas in 1999 and 2000. Instead of relying on emotional reactions, use an Investment Policy Statement that outlines your target investments in particular areas and creates a disciplined approach to investing.

2. Accept that you may not know as much as you think you know. Overconfident investors trade more and make more aggressive bets because they think they have better information than the market. The reality is that not many individuals, much less professional money managers, can outperform the market. What really works is a disciplined approach to investing over the long term.

3. Stick with your good choices longer, admit mistakes and dump them sooner. That's actually something we should apply in all areas of our lives! Back to that concept of irrational behavior. The quicker you can admit a mistake and change course, the quicker you can get back on track. Above all, remember successful money management and retirement planning is a marathon, not a 100-meter dash.

Have you observed emotional investing tendencies in any decisions that you have made? Make a note of them and steps you will take in the future to avoid, or record some principals to guide yourself to sound long term planning and investing in the future:

1. _____

2. _____

3. _____

# Day 28

## Nobody has the Secret Except You— Save and Follow a Disciplined Plan

*"The economy depends about as much on economists as the weather does on weather forecasters."*
*~Jean-Paul Kauffmann*

On any weekday morning, my alarm begins to blare at 4:45 a.m. sharp. Although it may take me a while to actually migrate from bed to shower, I always turn on CNBC as an encouragement to get moving. Through the years since my transition from business owner to financial advisor I have been increasingly amused by the prognosticators, the specialists, the economists, the elite hedge fund managers, the chartered financial analysts and the good looking anchors all sharing their tips to help the viewer either get into the market while the getting is good or get out of the market while they can! It seems to be either or and no in-between. If it's business as usual every morning on the TV, then there's my motivation to get going for another day of guiding and advising. My clue that I should lounge in bed for a few hours will be the day I hear one of those commentators announce that the secret is out-- save, follow a disciplined plan, use common sense and you too can plan your retirement.

The proliferation of expert information inundating the average investor through television, internet, news sources and literature is a twenty-four-hour, seven-days-a-week stream of hope, excitement, fear and crisis. Even if one has taken the time to analyze his legacy goals, create a financial plan, and follow an Investment Policy Statement, a torrent of information and contrary analysis can derail the best laid commitments and plans. I've witnessed intelligent investors leveraging their retirement nest eggs with information from Internet research and recommendations from economic entertainers whose specialty is not financial planning but high viewer ratings.

The dilemma of an abundance of information is the lack of accompanying context and the knowledge of how to interpret it. The key to freeing yourself from emotionally based decision-making without context is this: unplug the flow of information and rewire your brain with the lens of history. This last year the death march song was parroted endlessly about the collapse of the global financial system. While it was certainly a significant correction to the financial sector, one only has to look back ten years for the last "end of the world" financial crisis (Long Term Capital Management Crisis) and then look back another ten years for the "crisis to end all crisis" (Savings and Loans failures). Understanding that our world economy and financial system have many interlocking checks and balances, and that it is in the best interests of every country to sort out solutions can add a certain philosophical calmness when viewing the daily volatility of one's investment plans. As for knowledge of how to interpret the plethora of facts, unless one has the capability to translate a range of potentially unrelated data regarding the financial system, forward earnings of companies, macro economics and the market; then apply it to a disciplined long term investment philosophy, the daily, weekly and even yearly news cycle is useless and dangerous to your future dreams and goals. As you can imagine, nothing in the last paragraph will make a headline or sell a newspaper!

At this point you either have your financial roadmap in hand, or are in the process of creating one. Your carefully crafted plan will give you the insulation to continue to save and invest in a society where beliefs and feelings overshadow reality and accountability. Armed with a solid plan and a contextual and analytical viewpoint to long term investing, you will not be disarmed by the savvy investment newsletter promising safety from the upcoming Armageddon and safe profits--if you only buy a subscription. You will not feel doubtful upon hearing your plumber share the 1,000 percent profit made in penny stocks. And above all, you will always stick to the most commonly accepted and substantiated path to prudent retirement planning, no matter how boring it might sometimes seem!

In order to change my behavior in the future I vow to consult my life-map (Investment Plan and Investment Policy Statement) before making detours. I will record the top three goals of either my Investment Policy Statement or Investment Plan as a reminder of the path I will follow, even when the unexpected happens:

Instead rely on:

1. _____

2. _____

3. _____

# Day 29

# How the Market Really Works – 10 Percent a Year is a Big Fat Myth!

*"As securities rise, the perception of risk tends to gradually fade, until at a market peak, it seems like an artifact from an ancient civilization. But as soon as the markets crack, it's suddenly the driving investment thesis, as investors scramble towards safety"*
*~ Madison Investment Advisors, Inc. Winter 2008*

As a young entrepreneur, I was always looking at different sorts of businesses and ideas. At one time I found myself completely infatuated with the idea of running my own business at a ski resort. I had the opportunity to research some of the companies for sale in the area and saw that it had made a healthy profit over the past three years. "Sounds perfect!" I thought. After a few weeks of research I sat down and took a closer look at those income statements. I found that if I had owned the company for the past three years I would have spent twenty months with zero income, six months with out of this world profits and then ten months at a loss (all snow dependent, imagine that!). Once I considered the reality of using an unknown six months of income to tide me over for the other two and a half years, I was done skiing and headed back down to the flatlands. In life, if many choices were presented to us that way, we would most likely say no, unless of course we were one of those lucky ski bums with a trust fund.

Well, here's the rub. Stock market returns are just like the volatile returns of that fancy little business I dreamed of owning. Every time an individual, a financial planner, or a financial products marketer starts showing actual returns, they are all over the map. The only sane way to evaluate a long-term return is to annualize a return over time to get an accurate read of where one might end up a few years down the road. Thus when you read a study that illustrates the popular S&P 500 index has returned a tad over 10 percent over the long run (1926–2006), we each instantly visualize our nest egg happily growing fatter by 10 percent every single year. The reassurance of this marvelous investment plan is such that most people take that as a guarantee and when actual stock market returns kick in, the primal instinct we discussed in behavioral finance grabs the remaining money and runs for the hills. The truth is, only one year, 1971 had a return of around 10 percent (it was actually 10.8 percent). Almost any long term average samples of the S&P 500 performance are the product of nearly each year being above or below 10 percent, and usually by quite a bit. The average annual trading range is about 24 percent. Stop and picture that! That means, on average, stock market returns can vary year to year from low point to high point by 24 percent.

Here are some examples of yearly returns from the same time period that produced that 10 percent annualized return[3].

| | |
|---|---|
| 1933 | +47% |
| 1995 | +34% |
| 1997 | +31% |
| 1989 | +27% |
| 1973 | -17% |
| 2002 | -23% |
| 1974 | -30% |
| 1931 | -47% |

---

[3] Investors cannot directly purchase any index.

I once knew of an investor who would without fail call in on the worst day of the stock market, announce that all of the bad news and his instincts were telling him to get out of the doomsday market and sell each and every one of his stock holdings. As the investor's advisor worked patiently to educate the client on the profound damage he was incurring to his investment portfolio by selling when stocks were at their cheapest and then buying those same holdings after they had gone back up in price, he found that the investor had lost nearly seven years of retirement income from his portfolio that would be difficult to ever regain.

Staying the course with your investment plan could turn out to be one of the most vital decisions you make in regard to meeting your legacy goals. Even as I have internalized and witnessed these realities about the unpredictable changes that can occur in the stock market, I too go through times where I feel doubt and fear. Again, re-wire your perception so it is framed by history. The truth is, the biggest thing we have to fear are the consequences of our own actions creating unpredictable changes in our investment and financial plans.

The money **will** follow if we focus on that which is most important to us. Reaching our personal goals and dreams, both financially and in all areas of our life is possible when we frame every daily habit and decision within the context of whether it supports the ultimate realization of our legacies. Building a strong foundation to support ones legacy will be a lifetime commitment of sound and prudent financial planning with priceless results!

# Visit Tamaborriello.com for more helpful resources to help you change your finances forever